MW00677538

31 Days to Radically Reduce Your Expenses

31 Days to Radically Reduce Your Expenses: Less Stress. More Savings
Kalyn Brooke | CreativeSavingsBlog.com
Copyright © 2016

All Rights Reserved.

No part of this document may be reproduced or transmitted in any
form without prior written consent from the author.

ISBN 978-0-9971376-0-6 {Paperback}

ISBN 978-0-9971376-1-3 {Digital}

Disclaimer:

The advice and strategies contained herein may not be suitable for
your situation. You should consult with a professional where appropriate. Neither the publisher nor author shall be liable for any loss of
profit or any other commercial damages, including but not limited to
special, incidental, consequential, or other damages.

Due to the dynamic nature of the Internet, certain links and website information contained in this publication may have changed. The author
and publisher make no representations to the current accuracy of the
web information shared.

Published by KB Creative Media

Janna Madsen, Editor

Publishing and Design Services | MelindaMartin.me

31 Days to Radically Reduce Your Expenses

Less Stress. More Savings.

Kalyn Brooke

CreativeSavingsBlog.com

CREATIVE
media

TABLE OF CONTENTS

INTRODUCTION

By far, the biggest budgeting challenge is learning how to spend less. Not just in the little things here and there—we can easily skip buying a latte, cute top, or new throw pillow with some semblance of self-control, but it's also learning how to save on the big things too, like housing payments, utility bills, and those dreaded insurance premiums!

It's quite overwhelming when you start to think about how many things you actually pay for. Every year, it seems my own budget grows larger just to accommodate all the extra things we've added to it. There's always a new subscription service to try, a monthly membership to add, or a brand new décor piece begging you to take it home. But hey, at least we're budgeting for it, right?

The problem is, with all these costs eating up the majority of our income, there's very little left over to put towards something greater down the road. We're sacrificing future opportunities and savings goals in exchange for the most demanding "needs" and "wants" right now. Not to mention the unexpected medical bills and major repairs that happen at the worst time possible.

I can't even begin to tell you how many times we've had a water heater break the same week we replaced the tires on our car, and then on top of that, we find a leak under the sink from a faucet my husband Joseph just repaired. It sends us right back to the starting line, sometimes further behind than when we first began, and yes, it's totally frustrating! Especially when we have a mortgage to pay and food to put on the table on top of everything else.

That's why it's so important to make sure these necessary expenses—the bills you absolutely must pay—are also the least stressful. Because if we don't pay attention to how much we spend on the things we *need*, we'll never make room for the things we actually *want*.

A LIFE-CHANGING PRINCIPLE

It's awfully easy to look at your income and argue that life would be easier if you just made a little bit more. And it might...for a single moment. But have you ever heard of Parkinson's Law[1]? In technical terms, this principle says that work expands to fill the time available for its completion. In more basic language, it means the time spent is equal to what you have.

When we apply Parkinson's Law in a financial sense, we see that higher income often leads to higher expenses. Not because we intentionally set out to spend more, instead the extra money in our pocket gives us a false sense of security and more of a reason not to care. Why hold back when you have enough to afford it anyway?

But truthfully, more income doesn't solve the underlying issue. The idea of more means we're not content with what we have, and we don't believe that it's quite enough. When in reality, we already have everything we could possibly need. We just need to learn how to handle it in a completely different way.

So here's a question for you—instead of viewing your expenses as a frustration, **what if you used them as motivation to manage what you already have, *even better*?**

Just think of the savings potential! So much of our money washes away because we secretly believe the price of goods and services we pay for is unchangeable. When in reality, we've had the power all along to make this change ourselves. It starts with plugging up those tiny cracks—our monthly expenses—that if left unattended, can turn into some pretty big leaks.

IF YOU'VE ALREADY SACRIFICED SO MUCH

For some of you, your budget is already stretched as far as it can go, and you struggle with not knowing what else to cut. How do you manage your money when there's not much of it to manage in the first place? This is an incredibly hard place to be—trust me, I know! I've experienced my fair share of really hard times over the years, and it's overwhelming, stressful, and frustrating to say the least.

In fact, while I was writing this book, Joseph and I experienced one of the most trying years of our marriage. We had our first job loss, months of vacancy on the house we rent out in Upstate NY, and an expensive hospital bill that took us months to pay off. I say all that not for you to feel bad for us, but because it forced us to look at our budget, cut out a lot of unnecessary items, and really put into practice everything I talk about in the coming pages.

While a hard financial situation can feel paralyzing at the moment, now's the time when it's most crucial to act. You have to form a plan. For us, we methodically went through all of our expenses, one by one, to see what would make the biggest difference. We trimmed a lot of fat, found a few leaks, and lowered bills that we previously thought would barely make a dent. Because of this experience, I truly believe *every* expense always deserves a second look!

Think about this—how would your life change if:

- You shaved an extra $75 a month off your grocery bill?
- You found an extra $40 a month by switching phone carriers?
- You whittled down your car insurance by $25 a month with one simple phone call?

This is the potential *31 Days to Radically Reduce Your Expenses* has in store for you. And this time, you don't have to do it alone. Over the next 31 days, we'll walk through every single part of your budget together, take a hard look at what you're currently spending, and explore the tools and resources to change them for the better...even if you already think they're as low as they can go!

HOW TO READ THIS BOOK

Although the title suggests that you complete a chapter a day, one of the best parts about this book is that there's no requirement on how much time you spend on each section! You can read it from start to finish, or jump around based on the biggest expense or "pain point" you're experiencing right now. Then once you have at least one expense under control, choose another, and another, until you've lowered everything you possibly can.

I strongly suggest you have a highlighter and pen nearby. This isn't a book that you pick up, read, and never interact with or reference again. Remember, this is your expense-reducing guidebook! Each chapter has three action steps you can take right away, plus links to plenty of other resources to help support your journey.

I also encourage you to share your progress on social media using the hashtag #ReduceYourExpenses. Share a favorite tip or quote, and by all means, let me know how much you save! You never know who you might inspire to try *31 Days* themselves.

One last thing before we dive in—what you put into this process is what you'll ultimately get out of it. So if reducing your expenses in a radical way is important to you, take my suggestions, tips, and tricks, and put them into action as soon as you can. You're the one that has the power to make lasting change, and with this info-packed tool in your hands, you're going to be unstoppable!

I am excited for you to start your journey through *31 Days*. You'll quickly discover that more money at the end of the month is not just a pipe dream; it's finally a reality—one that moves you closer than ever before to the financial freedom you crave.

The only question is, are you ready?

Part 1: Reduce Housing Expenses

Day 1:
CHIP AWAY AT THAT MORTGAGE

If your mortgage payment is anything like mine, it probably takes up a pretty good portion of your budget. Buying a home is one of—if not *the*—biggest expense we will ever make, and this hefty bank payment leaves little left over at the end of the month for us to afford much of anything else!

But because it is the biggest, it also means we have the opportunity to make an even bigger impact if we lower or eliminate the payment entirely. I know what you're thinking right now—so much for easing into the whole reduce expenses thing, right?

It's true, this expense doesn't always have an immediate reward associated with it, but any opportunity to shorten the lifespan of your loan will literally pay off in the long run. Despite what you (and the banks) might think, your mortgage doesn't have to be a permanent fixture in your budget for the next thirty years. It's time to realize that you have control over those final numbers!

It took me years to start thinking this way. I loved saving money, but was perfectly content to be the responsible young adult who dutifully paid her mortgage every month, with little to no thought of how the bare minimum was affecting the rest of my bottom line. I wanted to give myself that extra cushion for the occasional eating out splurge, and still have enough for a yearly vacation after the rest of my bills were paid. Why sacrifice when you don't necessarily want to...or need to?

My wake-up call happened the first time I really looked at that end-of-year mortgage statement in the mail, and realized how much interest I was paying above and beyond the principal portion of my loan. If nothing else was going to motivate me to be completely debt-free, interest was doing a pretty good job on its own! I promised myself right then and there that I would do whatever steps necessary to pay my mortgage off as quickly as possible.

I know not everyone will consider their mortgage payment a priority, but I urge you to take a few minutes and imagine what your budget would look like if you didn't have a housing payment. Would you have an extra $800, $900, or $1,000 in your pocket? Once you envision all the things that money could go to rather than your mortgage, I think you'll kick yourself for not at least considering it. These ideas will help whittle down your payment, and make it a little more doable each month:

1. MAKE ONE EXTRA PAYMENT PER YEAR

Even if you don't do anything else, make just one extra principal payment every twelve months. Not only will you shave years off your loan, you'll also save thousands of dollars in interest. It's surprisingly easy to "find" extra money to put towards it too.

For instance, if you have a job that pays every two weeks, you receive 26 paychecks over the course of a year. Let's break it down even further and say you cover half your monthly mortgage payment from each paycheck, equaling 24 payments a year. That means you have two extra half payments to work with, or one full payment to put towards your mortgage!

Curious to know how much one payment actually saves? Here's an example:

Let's say you finance a home for $150,000 at a 4.5% interest rate for 30 years. Your monthly payment is $760.03. Over the life of the loan, you would pay a total of $273,610.07 to the bank.

But if you make one extra principal payment of $760.03 per year, you not only reduce your mortgage by 4 years and 7 months, but you also pay only $251,022.59—a total savings of $22,587.48—just for making one extra payment![2]

If making that extra payment at the end of the year seems daunting, talk to your bank to see if you can make payments every two weeks. You're essentially practicing the same method, but it's spread out over the course of an entire year instead of all at once.

JUST TO CLARIFY:

> **Principal Payment:** *Any payment that is made above and beyond your normal mortgage payment. It goes directly towards the amount owed on your home, not interest.*

2. KNOCK OUT PMI

Private Mortgage Insurance might not seem like much tacked on to your monthly payment, but it's still money you could be saving. Not quite sure you have PMI? Check with the bank where your loan is held, and they'll tell you the exact amount. But if you didn't have 20% to put down on your loan, you're probably paying it.

Making extra payments is one step closer to getting your PMI removed, and should be a huge incentive to work even harder. Once the PMI is gone, you could pay anywhere from $50-$100 less on your mortgage every month.

However, don't expect banks to keep track of this for you—I've heard stories of homeowners paying more PMI than they had to because they didn't stay on top of it. So keep track, and call your bank when you reach that 20% equity mark. I have a scrap piece of paper attached to my amortization schedule to remind me every time I make a payment.

3. CONSIDER REFINANCING

When interest rates are low, you may want to consider refinancing your home. Refinancing is just a fancy way of saying you get a brand new loan that pays off your old mortgage at a lower interest rate.

To do this, you *do* have to go through another round of closing costs, which could range anywhere between $3,000-$5,000, but this will ultimately reduce your monthly payment. Depending on how long you stay in the home, it could be worth the upfront cost.

Although I have not personally refinanced, I found a few *Creative Savings* readers who've already been through the process. Here's their advice:

> *We refinanced last year and that cut over $100 off our monthly payment! It was just in time since I am now a SAHM mom. We aim to make one extra pay-*

ment a year, oftentimes using our tax refund to do so.

— Kristen, joyfullythriving.com

We refinanced two years ago. We refinanced to the same term (30-year), but saved 2.25% interest and shaved $215 off our monthly payment. We're invest-ing the savings to build a home in a few years.

— Allison, MI

We refinanced to a 15-year so we could save tens of thousands on interest and finish paying before we retired.

— Amy, TX

4. HAVE YOUR PROPERTY REASSESSED

During the financial crisis of 2008, housing prices dropped considerably, triggering a domino effect that also lowered tax values. For those of us who have taxes included in our mortgage (also known as an escrow account), there's a good chance you can lower your monthly payment just by having your home reassessed.

Private companies offer these assessments for a fee, but it's actually quite easy to do yourself. Find a realtor to run "comps" on houses in your area, and compare those num-bers to your home's last assessed value. You can usually find this on your county's website under *property appraiser*. If the current value is significantly lower, call your local tax assessor and have them send you a form to fill out with your findings. The office will then determine whether or not your home is worth reevaluating.

This option is a little bit of a gamble as it really depends on what the current housing and real estate market looks like, but it's definitely worth researching!

5. FILE FOR A PROPERTY TAX EXEMPTION

Since we're on the subject of taxes, many states offer an exemption or credit on property taxes for residents who have lived in their home for at least a year.

Sometimes these exemptions are a flat rate, percentage of property value, or completely income based, but it really depends on what each specific state has to offer. While we have what is called a Homestead Exemption in Florida, we actually had a STAR Credit in New York. A call to your local tax commissioner or a quick Google search will bring up all the information you need to apply.

For those of you who live in Delaware, New Jersey, Rhode Island, Pennsylvania, and the District of Columbia, I'm sorry to say, but it doesn't look like there are any exemptions available in your area as of this writing. However, you may still be eligible for another kind of property tax incentive if you are over 65, disabled, or a veteran.

6. DOWNGRADE TO A SMALLER PROPERTY

It seems everyone is infatuated with the "tiny house movement" these days, and while I don't know that I could downsize and live in a house less than 600 square feet, there's something to be said about minimalistic living and its cumulative effect on money.

A smaller home most likely means a smaller mortgage payment, lower utilities, and less property taxes all around, so it's definitely worth considering if you don't need as much space. It doesn't necessarily have to be a house, either. Look into buying an airstream trailer, mobile home, RV, or manufactured home. I've even seen families live on a refurbished school bus!

Remember, when you commit to reducing debt, especially something as big as a mortgage, you must sacrifice some things in order to save. Analyze every purchase and eliminate anything that doesn't help you reach your goal. It's not always fun, but think of how much you'll be able to put towards that mortgage if you save every possible penny!

You'll also want to print out an amortization schedule as a tangible reminder of your payments. I do this for every loan we've ever had, and it's incredibly motivating to highlight each month as we pay it off. You can find a customizable amortization schedule at

CreativeSavingsBlog.com/Amortization

DAY 1 ACTION PLAN

- Adopt a savings mentality and try to make at least one extra payment per year.

- Explore alternative options, such as refinancing, reassessment, and tax exemptions.

- Print out an amortization schedule to keep track of payments.

Day 2:
REDUCE YOUR RENT

I'm a pretty picky person when it comes to apartments. They need to be located in a good part of town, and decently clean. Unfortunately, the small apartment Joseph and I moved to when we relocated to Florida was neither.

The price was quite reasonable compared to the other apartment complexes and condos offering oodles of services we didn't need, but I had a lot of scrubbing to do before we called it home, not to mention feeling just a tiny bit scared any time I ventured outside those four walls. Let's just say it wasn't uncommon to see the sheriff department's helicopter flying overhead!

Even though we wanted to buy a house as soon as possible, we needed this rental to help us through the transition period while we figured out exactly *what* house we wanted, and *where* we wanted to buy it.

As a renter, you might be in transition too—maybe you're saving towards a down payment, or renting because it allows you the flexibility to move in case a job takes you out of town. Or, you could be perfectly content to continue renting for as long as you need, avoiding those expensive home repairs and maintenance we homeowners have to deal with on a monthly, sometimes weekly, basis.

No matter your reasoning for pursuing the rental lifestyle, months of payments can feel just like a mortgage, minus the added benefit of equity. And what do you do when the price increases, year after year? Unless you have a great relationship with your landlord, this expense is one that has nowhere to go but up. Here's how to reverse the trend:

1. DO YOUR RESEARCH

Don't ever think rent is non-negotiable, because it always is! The worst your landlord can say is "No," so it's certainly worth a try. Take time to research the rental market for yourself, and be well-informed of the going rate in your area before you ever sign a contract. If you've been looking at a few rentals already, you probably have an idea of what's out there and for how much.

Don't forget to take the number of bedrooms into consideration too, as well as the location. Rentals fluctuate in price depending on quality, so be sure to compare similar apartments in similar neighborhoods.

If you're already renting a condo, room, or home, consider submitting a proposal to your landlord with your research findings. Hard stats will be the best negotiating tool you can offer. If they can't meet your request, have a thirty-day notice ready to submit, and be willing to go through with it. The landlord may decide that a vacancy is worse than lower rent and allow a decrease in payment, but use this tactic with caution. If you push too much below market value, you may find yourself out of a place to live!

2. SIGN AN EXTENDED LEASE

This doesn't work all the time, but if you plan to stick around for a while, try to negotiate a two or three-year lease for less. Speaking as a landlord myself, it's tough trying to find a reputable person to rent. I would much rather have a great tenant with an equally great credit score renting for longer at a lower price, than experience weeks and months of vacancy without pay.

If you are financially able, you could offer a certain number of payments in advance for a reduction in the monthly price. Many landlords are more than just one-time investors, and the extra cash would be a tempting incentive for those who have their eye on another property. They also love not having to worry about whether or not the rent will arrive on time.

3. RENT A DIFFERENT UNIT

Depending on the apartment complex, condominium, or multi-family home, there's a possibility that certain units cost more as a result of newer features, while others with older carpeting and dated cabinets rent for much less.

This is how our rental property in New York is set up. The home has both a top and bottom apartment with the exact same floor plan, but the top unit includes an additional finished attic that adds extra square footage to the space. Logically, it rents for more than the bottom one.

The type of upgrades and specific part of the complex will be your deciding factor in payments, but you could shave anywhere from $10-$100 off your monthly rent simply by asking if there's an alternative option.

READER TIP:

At our current complex, I purposely chose the UN-upgraded unit as it is all carpet and tile with NO hardwood/laminate. We have dogs and I don't want *to get dinged on move-out due to scratches in the flooring from their paws. The entire rest of our unit is super nice and we love the complex. By choosing the non-upgraded unit, I save $30/mo on my rent and the location of our unit within the complex saves us another $10.*

—*Mary, GA*

4. OFFER YOUR ASSISTANCE

All landlords have projects they need to get done around the property, and it never hurts to ask how you can help in exchange for a discount on rent.

Sometimes it's a one-time repair, while others require daily or weekly maintenance. As long as you're a hard worker and willing to learn, many property owners would jump at the chance for extra help. Some of the most common tasks to outsource are yardwork, painting, plumbing, or just keeping an eye on things.

If you do take an occasional odd job, talk beforehand with your landlord to nail down how payment will work. Will it be strictly reimbursement based, or per project? Will they subtract the amount from rent, or pay you via cash or check? It's good to have an agreement like this in writing to protect both parties. You'll also want to save any receipts used to repair or maintain the property, and keep good records in case a disagreement ever arises.

5. BRING IN A ROOMMATE

If subletting is allowed, see if you can bring in a roommate to offset costs. Some landlords may add a fee for extra utility usage, but the benefits might be worth the added expense.

The best option to find a roommate is to check with friends or family members who are in transition and need a place to crash for a few months. For those that don't mind rooming with a stranger, Roommates.com can send you potential matches. Just make sure your spouse or significant other is on board before offering an invite.

If you do find someone who is willing to split the rent, there's actually one of two ways to make an agreement. Either divide everything equally between the two (bills, rent, food, etc.), or sublet and rent the place to your roommate. This means you pay for everything, but charge your roommate a set amount. Both work, but if you're looking for less hassle and fewer arguments, choose the latter. Be very careful, though, as subletting is commonly prohibited in many leases.

6. FIND ANOTHER PLACE

If all else fails and you're not able to handle your monthly payment anymore, you should probably look for another place. I know how much of a pain it is to move, but if you can save $100/month and plan on renting for at least another year, that's $1,200 in savings!

The best places to look for apartments online are Craigslist, Trulia, and Zillow. You can also check your local paper, and of course, collect recommendations from friends and family. Keep surrounding towns and cities in mind too—a less expensive area might have a longer commute, but the trade-off could be worth it depending on price.

You should also note what expenses are included before making a final decision. A property might have lower rent, but if it doesn't have utilities, cable, or any other amenities included in the price, it could be more expensive in the long run.

READER TIP:

My husband and I owned a home before making an out-of-state move for his job a while back. We chose a two-bedroom apartment that was news construction and in a very nice area. After a couple years, we decided to move to a cheaper townhouse that didn't have all the amenities (pool, fitness center, etc.) and was not big by any means (1,000 sq. ft.), but was still in an area we were very comfortable and safe in for a short-term transition. This saved us an additional $200 per month on rent for the next three years while we saved and waited for the right time to buy our house.

—Cherie, VA

7. CONSIDER RENTER'S INSURANCE

I know we're discussing how to reduce expenses, but I couldn't finish out this chapter without at least mentioning renter's insurance. Yes, it's an added cost, but if catastrophic damage from a possible flood, fire, tornado, or theft actually happened, you would need to replace all your belongings, which can add up rather quickly depending on how much you have and how expensive it is. In fact, some complexes even require renter's insurance before they let you live there!

A typical policy starts as low as $12/month, and some will even cover hotel stays, temporary rentals, and meals if you are displaced from your home. You'll most likely have to pay a deductible if you do ever file a claim, but the cost of that will solely depend on your premium.

Then again, you can always risk it and assume that nothing bad would ever happen, but that, of course, is completely up to you. I've already been through one flood, so I don't consider anything to be off limits!

Many of these options require negotiation on your part, but even if your landlord says no, it doesn't hurt to put yourself out there and ask. Just remember to be kind, confident, and respectful during every conversation—you never know when they might give you a break!

DAY 2 ACTION PLAN

- Research average rental prices for your area, and depending on what you find, talk with your future or current landlord about a reduction in price.

- Request lower rent in exchange for advanced payments or help around the property.

- Consider alternative methods to offset costs, such as bringing on a roommate or moving into a different unit.

Day 3:
LOWER THE COST OF HOME REPAIRS

Benjamin Franklin once said, "In this world nothing can be said to be certain, except death and taxes."[3] But for those of us who are homeowners, I'd like to add one more item to his short list—*home repairs.*

Unfortunately, this is one aspect of homeownership we often like to ignore. As starry-eyed first-time homebuyers, it's hard to see past the idea of our dream home, and what it means to take care of it. But *all* houses, whether they're a 100-year-old farmhouse or brand new and custom-built, are going to have items to repair, fix, or replace. And depending on the type of project or how bad the damage is, your bank account can take quite the beating trying to keep up with them all, especially since they almost always seem to happen within just a few weeks of each other!

The best way to soften the blow of an emergency home repair is to have what is commonly known as an Emergency Fund, or you could also call it a Home Repair and Maintenance Fund. This is basically a "rainy day" savings account that won't allow unexpected repairs to completely destroy your budget, because you already have money set aside for it.

The typical amount to start with in an Emergency Fund is $1,000, which is a great goal if you're new to "emergency savings," but as a general rule, 1% of the home's assessed value per year will leave you with a comfortable amount for any potential issues that might happen. That means for a $150,000 home, you should set aside $1,500 per year or $125 per month.

I know what you're thinking right now—how do you find extra money when your budget is stretched as far as it can go? Trust me, I get it, but Emergency Funds are too important to ignore. And even if you can only manage $5 a week, that's better than nothing. You will feel so much better knowing you have a little bit extra stashed away for when that rainy day really pours!

However, since one single incident has the potential to completely wipe out your Emergency Fund, it's essential to stretch that money as far as it can go. Here's how to keep those unexpected repairs as low as possible:

1. DO-IT-YOURSELF

When something goes wrong, you can either call in an expert, or attempt to fix it yourself. Most of us tend to gravitate towards the latter, as the DIY route is typically viewed as the most budget-friendly option. And when you look at current labor costs, that's mostly true. It's hard to justify spending that money on a professional when you may have the skills needed to fix the problem yourself...and for much less!

READER TIP:

With our condo, we had recurring plumbing problems and every time we had to fork out €150 just for a plumber to show up. We got fed up with it and bought a plumbers spring to fix it ourselves. Saved us at least €500 and the spring cost a mere €10.

—Monique, Netherlands

We recently did this when the heating elements in our hot water heater rusted out from hard water. We could have called a plumber for $60 an hour, and crossed our fingers that he'd finish the job in that amount of time, or we could buy an $8 tool along with $22 worth of replacement parts, and attempt it ourselves. It actually only took Joseph two hours to complete the job, saving us at least $30.

If you don't know the exact steps to make a repair, but are pretty sure you or someone in your household has the skills to figure it out, don't be afraid to do a quick search on Google or YouTube for detailed instructions. There are thousands of tutorials available to guide you through almost any DIY attempt.

2. LEARN YOUR LIMITS

Being able to DIY is great, but you have to know your limits too. There are some things you simply won't be able to do yourself, and will cost a lot more money, time, and frustration in the long run if you go it alone.

Not sure when to DIY and when to hire out? Ask yourself these questions before making a final decision:

- Do I have the basic skills required to complete this project?

- How much time will it take me?

- How expensive are the tools needed? Is it possible to borrow or rent them?

- Do I feel completely confident I can complete this project without any (or very minimal) mistakes?
- What does my research tell me in terms of project difficulty? Is this something people normally hire out, or is it an easy DIY?
- What do the laws of my city or county allow me to do? (i.e., Do I need a permit?)

Depending on your answers, you may decide it's best to call a professional. They *are* called that for a reason!

3. USE CONTRACTORS YOU TRUST

When you call in a contractor, it is incredibly important to find and use one you trust. As frustrating as it is, there are handymen who scam their customers, do shoddy work, and profit from natural disasters with exorbitant price hikes. You do not want to be on the receiving end of one of them.

Even if you're not in the middle of a home repair right now, it's good to gather as many word-of-mouth contacts as you can to file away for later. Ask friends and family who they've used in the past and would recommend, and if you want to go a step further, check with the Better Business Bureau to see if there have been any recent complaints about the business you're inquiring about.

To reduce the amount spent on contractors, be sure to request multiple quotes from those contacts you just collected. And when there's a contractor who quotes a higher price, but makes you feel more comfortable, don't hesitate to show them the other quote and request a price match.

You should also ask for an itemized price list of the entire project, and see what you can do yourself to save money on the final total. We removed and disposed of our own carpet before asking the installers to come, which saved us $100!

READER TIP:

We recently had a plumbing problem that required digging out the yard and replacing part of the line hooking into the city's mainline. We had quotes of $6,000+, but were fortunate to find a local guy who did it for $1,500.

—Jody, NE

4. BARTER FOR HELP

Sometimes you have a project that isn't complex enough to call in a contractor, but you're still not comfortable handling it all by yourself. That's when skilled friends come in handy!

Put out a request on Facebook or check with friends that can help with whatever you need done—woodwork, drywall, plumbing, etc. Many will do so just to be a "good neighbor," and only require a hot meal, plenty of water, and an occasional batch of cookies in exchange. But if you want to go a step further, buy your friend a gift card to eat out on your tab, and always be ready to lend a hand with whatever skills you might have when they are in need themselves.

5. BUY RELIABLE REPLACEMENTS

When you *do* have to buy a replacement part, whether it's a new faucet, fridge, or even something as big as an air conditioner, it pays to research your options. Even though it might be tempting to buy the least expensive brand, cheap fixtures don't always last.

Read multiple reviews from a variety of sources and ask around to see what friends and family have used themselves. It's much better to pay for a replacement part that lasts ten to twenty years, than to skimp on one that lasts only two. You'll only end up paying more money in the long run.

6. PERFORM PREVENTATIVE MAINTENANCE

Preventative maintenance is the best way to keep outrageous repairs from taking over your home. No, you won't be able to stop every possible problem from happening, but by doing simple tasks such as changing your air conditioner and/or furnace filters often, preventing water leaks with caulk, and regularly cleaning out gutters, you will significantly reduce the chance of even bigger problems down the road.

Also, if you love to-do lists and schedules, put some of the most common maintenance items into a checklist so you can keep up on all that preventative maintenance without it slipping your mind. Staying organized is key to things getting done, and you can download a Home Maintenance Checklist at CreativeSavingsBlog.com/ExpenseResources to make sure you never forget another task.

You don't need to be afraid of expensive home repairs, but it's smart not to underestimate them either. Be prepared with an emergency reserve, and always look for ways to cut costs throughout the process!

DAY 3 ACTION PLAN

- If you don't have an emergency fund yet, decide on a monetary goal and commit a specific amount every week to fund it as soon as possible.

- Collect a variety of trustworthy contacts to keep on hand if and when you're hit with another unexpected repair.

- Print out and use a Home Maintenance Checklist to keep your home running smoothly and avoid potential issues down the road.

Day 4:
REPLACE BIG-TICKET ITEMS FOR LESS

When Joseph and I moved into our new home last year, we envisioned a wrought iron patio set on the lanai, a cozy king bed for the master bedroom, and the perfect arrangement of couches, loveseats, and chairs to entertain guests. The only problem was, after the down payment, we didn't have any extra money in the budget to make any of those purchases. It was overwhelming to decide what to save for and how to start!

You might think a new furniture set, mattress, large appliances, and electronics shouldn't be considered a monthly expense; however, they do creep into our budgets at various times throughout the year. Whether an item is old and needs replacing, or you finally have enough money saved up to splurge on something shiny and new, you have to be prepared for these one-time expenses just as much as your monthly ones. A little bit of research in the beginning, as well as close attention to shifting prices, will help you make the best possible purchase.

Whenever I feel overwhelmed by all the things I need or want to buy, I make a Household Wish List. It doesn't matter whether you have the money to buy everything on that list right now—that's why it's called a wish list! This short exercise transfers all your wants and needs from brain to paper, so you can see everything you'd like to buy in one glance.

Once you have your list, pull out a clean sheet of paper and write down each item in the order you want (or need) to purchase it. If you have a spouse, schedule a date night at home and talk over this list together, then label accordingly. For structure to help fill in those blanks, you can download a Household Wish List at

CreativeSavingsBlog.com/ExpenseResources

The items you write down may or may not be purchases you need to make right away, so depending on the timetable, you have some time to find *exactly* what you want—which is usually how I prefer to shop anyway!

You can also use this time to start a separate savings account for any big-ticket item on your list. This keeps your money away from regular bills and expenses, and allows you to focus much better on reaching that one financial goal.

Then, when you're finally ready to commit to a big expense, refer to the list below for the best ways to start your search, and how to find the lowest price possible.

1. SEARCH CRAIGSLIST EVERY DAY

Craigslist is a fantastic place to find all sorts of used furniture and appliances, but you have to be patient and check every day to find exactly what you're looking for. I didn't always enjoy browsing through Craigslist—I thought the interface was ugly and cumbersome (FYI: it still is), and hated the thought of dealing with not-so-trustworthy individuals who thought scamming (and kidnapping) people was fun. Clearly, I've watched too many movies! But now that I've learned how to manage Craigslist well, it's one of the first online resources I refer to.

To get the best use out of Craigslist, begin your search under the Owner category (not Dealer), and ask lots of questions before meeting someone to pick up your item. This will save you from wasted time and the hassle of actually seeing the item in person, then deciding that you don't want it because you didn't ask for sizes or other vital information.

What sort of questions should you ask? I always start with these four:

- What are the measurements or size of this piece? (if referring to furniture)

- What is the exact model number? (if referring to an appliance)

- Does this item come from a smoke-free home?

- How old is this item?

A word of warning: You must be incredibly careful setting up an exchange. If the transaction has to be done at home, have a spouse or friend with you when the buyer arrives. Otherwise, I suggest that you meet in a public place for extra protection.

READER TIP:

Find the exact model you want, and set up alerts on Craigslist, then earmark a certain amount of money to be transferred into an online savings account each month. I did this last summer with our new couch. I originally planned on spending $600, but (surprise!) paid only $250 for a brand new couch with free delivery and takeaway.

—Kelsey, WA

2. SHOP USED RETAILERS

Surprisingly, thrift stores, consignment shops, and flea markets don't just sell worn out clothes and chintzy items—they almost always have a section of the store with used furniture. Not all items will be in perfect condition, but if you have a little imagination and a lot of paint, these beasts can quickly turn into bona fide beauties.

While searching online for kitchen counter stools, I found a gorgeous set that was the exact style and color I wanted, but they cost over $100 apiece. I couldn't bring myself to buy them and instead, waited to see if anything close to what I was looking for popped up in our local thrift store. On a day when I least expected it, two beautiful stools arrived at $20 each, and were almost identical to the ones I'd been eyeing. They weren't the exact color I wanted (black instead of white), but I knew painting them would be an easy fix.

Try to look past cosmetics on any piece, whether you pick it up at a thrift store or on the side of the road. You can almost always paint, refinish, or reupholster it. And if you need any newbie furniture makeover and finishing tips, you'll find a collection of helpful resources at

Pinterest.com/CreativeSavings/Decorating-101

3. STOP BY SCRATCH AND DENT STORES

If you're not especially picky about a tiny scratch, stain, or tear, don't forget to check your local scratch and dent stores for discounted brand-name items. These items often get damaged during shipping, and companies don't necessarily want to sell them right next to their regular offerings.

The great thing about scratch and dent is it gives those of us looking for a great deal a chance to buy almost brand new for less. And who knows, you might find that perfect piece, and no one will probably notice anything wrong with it!

You'll have better luck finding chain store scratch and dents rather than small and family-owned, but it doesn't hurt to call around to see if local furniture or appliance stores have a nearby outlet. You can also visit SearsOutlet.com and ApplianceSmart.com if you're comfortable buying online—just be sure to know your prices beforehand (and check your shipping costs) so you don't overpay.

READER TIP:

IKEA has a big corner near the checkout area with demos and slightly scratched items that go for rock bottom.

—*Monique, Netherlands*

4. BROWSE YARD AND MOVING SALES

Because most homeowners, including myself, have way too much stuff lying around, yard and moving sales are the perfect place to find new-to-you treasures. Check Craigslist or your local paper for exact times, or go out for an early drive Friday or Saturday morning to find unadvertised gems and browse the best selection. The cliché "the early bird gets the worm" is almost always true when shopping an early morning garage sale!

Estate sales run in a similar way to garage sales, but beware of higher prices when shopping one. I stopped by my first estate sale earlier this year and was shocked by how much everything cost. I later learned that private companies usually manage the family's belongings, and an extra middleman means you don't get as great of a deal. I still wouldn't be afraid to try to negotiate a better price, though—it certainly doesn't hurt!

Local Facebook sales groups are another great place to look for used big-ticket items, and you can do that from the comfort of your own home. Just type "virtual yard sale" or "garage sale" into the search box on Facebook along with your closest town, city, or county for a list of groups near you. Another perk is the ability to list anything you want to sell too.

5. PLAN PURCHASES AROUND SEASONAL SALES

Although you can't always "schedule" an exact time to buy a big-ticket item, it's still smart to have an idea of when the typical seasonal sales are and how long they last. Here's a peek at current sales trends during each month so you know when the best prices take effect:

January: Fitness Equipment & TVs

February: Indoor Furniture

March: Electronics & Cameras

April: Lawn Tools & Equipment

May: Camping/Outdoor Gear & Mattresses

June: Indoor Furniture & Computers

July: Indoor/Outdoor Furniture

August: Outdoor Furniture & Air Conditioners

September: Grills, Bikes, & Lawn Equipment

October: Electronics & Cars

November: Electronics & Appliances

December: Electronics & Appliances

Also, I know Black Friday makes some of us cringe, but *so* many items are on sale that day that it's sometimes worth the extra hassle to find a steal. You never know...you might just discover an amazingly low price in the middle of all those crowds!

6. SKIP THE EXTENDED WARRANTY

If you do end up buying new instead of used, you probably don't need to add an extended warranty to your purchase. In fact, I would strongly encourage you not to buy one, and focus on reliability instead. An item that lasts for decades won't need to be replaced.

Many credit cards also offer a one-year or double-extended warranty in addition to the manufacturer's guarantee. Check with your credit card company to see if this is listed in the agreement or as one of their added benefits, and keep track of all the original documents and receipts in a separate file folder in case you need to file a claim. Your due diligence could get your item replaced for free!

As you make your Household Wish List and begin your search, remember, patience is key. You can save hundreds just by waiting for the right time to buy, and it's worth holding off to find that perfect piece for much less.

But let's say you don't find exactly what you want—am I asking you to compromise? Not at all. Start saving for that big-ticket item, and pay full price if you have to, but do it only after working it into your budget just like any other monthly expense.

DAY 4 ACTION PLAN:

- Download and fill out a Household Wish List, then determine your top three purchases.

- Start a separate savings account for one item you would like to save up for, then set aside a specific amount every week to go towards it.

- Begin browsing Craigslist, used retailers, and yard sales with purpose, and always keep an eye out for items on your wish list!

Day 5:
LOWER YOUR HOME INSURANCE POLICY

Neither of us wants to think about needing home insurance, but as we've already discussed in the chapter about home repairs, a lot can go wrong when you own such a big asset. Accidental fires, stolen property, potential floods, and other natural disasters (some even requiring additional policies), make your home sound like a house of straw from a fairy tale, rather than a protective fortress!

I think we can all agree that homeowner's insurance is a good idea. Some of us may not have a choice in the matter (banks require insurance if you hold a mortgage), but very few would ever consider *not* having it at all.

The problem lies in knowing how much to spend versus the amount of coverage or protection we need. Because when you break it down, home insurance is mainly a matter of risk. We're betting that any potential house issues will be covered by insurance, while the insurance company is betting we will rarely need to use the policy we signed up for. The crucial point is finding a balance of both coverage and cost, and there are a lot of variables at play in deciding exactly where that middle ground is.

In preparing for this chapter, I read a lot of articles encouraging homeowners just to drop unnecessary coverage in order to reach that perfect balance. Seems reasonable, right? But after talking extensively with an independent insurance agent to verify this, I discovered it's not that simple. Most companies already start your policy at the lowest insurance limits they allow, and much of what is covered is already included as one flat rate, or as a percentage of your home's value.

So is there any hope in lowering your home insurance? You bet! It might seem like you can't control the price the same way you can with your grocery bill or clothing budget, but there are still a few ways to make sure your policy is the lowest it can go without sacrificing necessary coverage.

1. UNDERSTAND YOUR POLICY

I am horrible at reading the fine print, especially on something as boring as homeowner's insurance, but understanding your policy is the first step to any legitimate savings. You can't know what to save on if you have no idea what's covered in the first place!

Of course, coverage varies depending on your specific policy, but typically, these items are almost always included:

- Your home (and an attached garage) in the event that either is damaged
- Other structures on the property (e.g., shed)
- Contents inside your home and other structures
- Lodging in case your home becomes uninhabitable
- Personal liability and financial protection in case someone is injured on your property

Items not usually covered:
- Flooding
- Sewer Backups
- Sinkholes
- Termite Infestation
- Acts of Terrorism
- Nuclear Plant Accidents

I made a very costly mistake in assuming that flooding was covered in our home insurance policy, so imagine my surprise when we experienced our first flood! Now I make it a point to understand exactly what I pay for, and it's a good habit to get into not just for home insurance, but for other types of insurance as well.

If you're having trouble deciphering your insurance policy, call the insurance company and have them walk you through step-by-step. Don't be afraid to ask questions! Most companies are happy to help interpret any foreign terms or insurance jargon, and this process will give you a good idea of how much you're spending each year based on how much protection you actually have.

2. SHOP WITH AN INDEPENDENT AGENT

If there's only one thing you choose to do to save on homeowner's insurance, let it be this—don't exclusively approach or work with one specific brand. I have continually received the best deals by working with an independent insurance agent, someone who isn't loyal to any particular company. They are like covert operatives working behind the scenes to find you the best deal, and they're FREE. Pretty cool, right?

Because these agents do all the legwork for you, you don't have to spend time gathering quotes by yourself, comparing coverage, and navigating uncharted insurance territory where nothing makes sense to those of us not trained in this area. This saves homeowners a lot of time, money, and headaches in the long run!

READER TIP:

The best way to find an agent you can trust is by word-of-mouth, so ask your friends who they use and recommend. TrustedChoice.com/Find-an-Agent and DaveRamsey.com/ELP are great sites to connect with a provider who is trained to find you the best coverage possible. We went with an independent agent and reduced our current policy by half. That, in turn, reduced our mortgage by half! It took a little effort but will save us $5,000 a year.

—Kathy, CA

3. CHOOSE A HIGH DEDUCTIBLE

A high deductible policy almost always results in a lower out-of-pocket premium; however, it also means you pay a higher amount if damage or theft were to happen to your home. It's a risky move with pros and cons on either side, but could potentially save you hundreds, if not thousands, of dollars in the long run.

Before you get too excited and call your insurance agent, you need to be positive this is the best move for you, your family, and the area you live in. If your location frequently has hurricanes, tornadoes, earthquakes, and/or wildfires, a higher deductible might not be the smartest decision. You should also have an Emergency Fund in place to cover the cost of the deductible, in case you ever *did* file a claim. You don't want to create even more financial strain on you and your family because you didn't have enough to meet it.

On the flip side, an Emergency Fund can also pay for repairs that may be cheaper to do yourself rather than pay the deductible and file a claim. Many insurance companies increase your premium if you file a claim (I know, it doesn't make sense), so you want to be very careful when deciding what to file and how often.

4. RESEARCH AVAILABLE DISCOUNTS

Depending on certain characteristics of your home, you as an individual, or by housing multiple insurance policies under the same roof, insurance companies may offer you an additional discount. Since all of these options have the potential to lower your overall rate, they're definitely worth asking about!

Here are the most common ways to earn discounts:

- Bundling your home, auto, and life insurance policies together
- Installing protective devices in your home (e.g., a security system or smoke detector)
- Buying a newly built or newly renovated home
- Not filing a claim
- Maintaining good credit
- Not smoking
- Being 55 or older

However, just because a company offers you a discount, doesn't always mean it's the best option. Some policies end up being more expensive than others, even though they have four or five discounts included. Focus on the final cost, and compare prices with other companies that may not offer a discount, but have less expensive options instead.

As much as I wish we could just "set it and forget it," homeowner's insurance is not a once-and-done kind of deal. You need to be your best advocate and stay on top of that rate. A simple annual evaluation before it's time to pay your next premium is worth putting on the calendar to make sure you're getting the lowest rate possible!

DAY 5 ACTION PLAN

- Call your insurance company and talk through your policy to make sure you understand what you're paying for.

- See if there is any way to lower it via a higher deductible, available discounts, or by allowing an independent insurance agent to find you a better deal.

- Mark your calendar one month before your home insurance expires, and see if any new options or discounts are available.

Part 2:
Reduce Car Expenses

Day 6:
SAVE BIG AT THE PUMP

As someone who enjoys routine and stability, fluctuating gas prices and I do not mix. Sometimes it spikes over $3 a gallon, while the next month we're seeing prices well under $2—often with no rhyme or reason besides a trending political news story.

I realize these prices are still pretty decent in America compared to other countries, but I think we can all agree there's a huge emotional component tied to watching gas prices dip and soar. Lack of consistency also means gas is difficult to budget for each month. Sure, we have other variable expenses, like groceries or clothing, that fluctuate depending on needs, but their semi-dependable pricing is much easier to plan around than fuel. This month, $150 in gas *may* be enough to get you where you need to go...next month, maybe not.

But until we find another resource to fuel our vehicles, or electric cars become more mainstream, there's not much we can do to prevent this painful purchase. Even though our world is more closely connected via technology than ever before, we don't all live in a metropolitan area within walking distance of our favorite stores. Nor do we always have the means to take advantage of public transportation like the subway, train, or the latest trendy obsession, Uber.

We *do*, however, have the power to maximize how far we travel on one tank of gas, and believe it or not, even control the price at which we fill up.

Here's how to drive further for much less, and make that tank last as long as possible!

1. STAY HOME

Seems like a no-brainer, but how many of us find an excuse to "run to the store" for "one quick thing"? As someone who works from home, I know how hard it is to be cooped up inside all day, but I also know the length between fill-ups increases substantially when you avoid an outing.

If you have a hard time staying home, these no-spend ideas are sure to keep you busy:

- Read a book
- Clean the house
- Clean the car
- Organize an area of your home
- Declutter and sell your items on Craigslist
- Make a yummy recipe or a DIY project you saved on Pinterest
- Learn a new skill
- Call a family member or friend you haven't talked to in a while
- Try a new hairstyle
- Make a card (or two or three)
- Go on a walk
- Ride your bike
- Start a blog

- Write in your journal
- Catch up on a TV series

If all else fails, you know that nagging to-do list you never have time to complete? Now's the perfect opportunity to cross some of those items off!

For those who work outside the home, it's worth asking your boss if there's any way you can telecommute a few days a week. This won't work for every profession, but you never know until you ask. Otherwise, see if you can catch a ride with a friend who lives nearby, or coordinate with a family member who heads out to work at the same time you do.

2. BATCH ERRANDS

When you do leave the house, be sure to run errands all at one time, and batch stores together based on location. This eliminates unnecessary travel, and doesn't just save gas money, but it also saves time.

The best way to avoid unnecessary trips is to keep a detailed grocery or supply list and whenever you're low on an item, write it down. I am the queen of unnecessary errands because I often run out of something I've forgotten to put on the list!

But if you do forget to pick up an ingredient for dinner that night, don't be afraid to get creative. I've saved many a meal just by searching for a substitution on Google, or changing dinner plans based on what we already had in the pantry.

READER TIP:

The two main saving strategies for our family are staying home and batching errands. It takes us several minutes to get to the freeway and to our main shopping center so we make sure we really need to go out before we head into town.

—*Julia, MN*

3. USE ALTERNATIVE TRANSPORTATION

Not all of us live near a downtown or metropolitan area, but for those who do, try walking or riding your bike the next time you need to get something. It will take a little bit longer to get where you need to go, but on the flipside, it's an opportunity to slow down in this fast-paced world and savor the everyday. It can also be a great way to get out of the house for a while and stretch your legs.

If you do decide to walk or ride your bike, try to have the proper equipment with you, such as a basket for your bike, or sturdy reusable bags to carry. I once lost a few cans of pasta sauce on my way home from the grocery store because the plastic ones couldn't carry all that weight!

The bus, train, subway, or carpooling with friends is another great way to get around town without using your vehicle. It might feel like you're losing a little bit of your independence when you have to rely on the schedule of a transportation company or friend/family member, but just a few trips per month make a pretty good dent in the gas budget.

4. TRACK AND COMPARE PRICES

The majority of gas stations have sale days when the gas is a few cents cheaper than regular prices. It's good practice to mentally track these prices (or write them down if needed) based on location, day, and at what station so you know the best time to fill up.

You can also download the GasBuddy app (available on iOS and Android), which displays up-to-date pricing information about gas stations near you. I wouldn't drive miles out of your way to save $.03 per gallon, but if you live in an area with access to multiple gas stations, it's worth doing a price comparison before you head out!

Another option is to use a warehouse club gas station. You won't necessarily earn rewards for buying your gas from them, but you do get anywhere from $.05-$.15 cheaper than other stations in town, just by being a member.

5. TAKE ADVANTAGE OF REWARDS

Many grocery stores offer a gas/grocery combination where you earn cents off the gallon based on how much you spend at that specific store. As of this writing, these stores currently participate in a gas rewards program:

- Giant
- Ingles
- Kroger
- Martin's
- Price Chopper
- Safeway
- Shop n' Save
- Weis Markets
- Winn Dixie

Shell offers a more generic Fuel Rewards program that allows everyday purchases to count towards fuel discounts. You also get $.03 off per gallon just for being a member, which means you never have to pay full price for gas again! You can learn more about this program at FuelRewards.com.

And lastly, if you have a credit card, see what the cash back percentage is on gas-only purchases (it's usually between 2-5%). You could earn an extra $100 per year just by paying for a commodity you need to buy anyway. If you are nervous about owning a credit card, a gas-only card makes it super simple to build credit and maintain much-needed discipline. Since you only charge for the fuel you use, it's pretty easy to avoid overspending. Just be sure to pay that bill in full, every month!

6. DRIVE SMARTER

The Internet has quite a few "gas saving hacks" that tell you driving slower, filling your tires to the appropriate pressure, or avoiding routes with extra stop signs and traffic lights will help your tank last longer.

Here's what the U.S. Department of Energy has to say[4]:

- Aggressive driving lowers your gas mileage by 33% on the highway, and 5% around town.

- Idling can use ¼-½ a gallon of fuel per hour. Any shutdown longer than 1 minute will save money. (e.g., school pickup lines)

- Tires inflated to the proper pressure increase gas mileage up to 3.3%.

- Using the manufacturer's recommended grade of motor oil improves gas mileage up to 2%.

- An extra 100 pounds of weight decreases gas mileage by only 1%.

The conclusion? Driving crazy isn't healthy for you or your car, and a smooth running vehicle gives the most fuel for your dollar.

You can try your best to save money on gas in every which way possible, but if you have a gas guzzler, it may be time to consider something more fuel efficient. It might not be a purchase you can afford right now, but keep it in mind for later (or as a separate savings fund), and do car-related research in the meantime. I love digging into Consumer Reports to find which vehicle gets the most miles per gallon.

DAY 6 ACTION PLAN:

- Download the GasBuddy app and track sales prices so you know when and where to fill up.

- Choose just one day this week to run all your errands.

- Focus on driving smarter in order to improve gas mileage, or find an alternative transportation option to get you where you need to go.

Day 7:
LOWER THE COST OF CAR REPAIRS

Ahhh...cars. Unless you live in the middle of a great big city, it's rare to meet a person without one. In fact, I can't imagine how different and much smaller our world would be without cars. I'll be the first to admit that I absolutely love the freedom and flexibility I get from owning my own vehicle, and how quickly it gets me to and from the store. Plus, it's fun to pack the trunk and speed off on a spontaneous road trip every once in a while!

But until you own a car for yourself, you never truly understand what a pain they are to manage, maintain, fill up, and repair. It doesn't matter whether you buy used or brand new—cars are not built to last more than a few decades, and those years are often filled with financial stress as we replace part after part to keep them running. It's no wonder cars are considered one of the worst investments you can ever make.

Joseph and I try to head off some of the more expensive repairs by keeping a little bit extra stashed away for those rainy days, but once that "domino effect" starts, it's hard to stop. One year we had a substantial tax return that we were thrilled to put towards a down payment on our first house. But right after we deposited the check, our transmission died, and that money we had been so excited about saving went straight to the local mechanic instead.

While I'm thankful we had that money when we did, it's proof that cars are very expensive pieces of equipment to maintain. However, I'm not about to give up my license to drive, or sell the very thing we use almost every day...are you? That means we have to figure out how to keep our vehicles as low maintenance (and inexpensive) as possible.

Since I'm not a car expert by any means, I peppered Joseph with questions about how we can save more on car maintenance and repairs. He was full of great advice, and here are the six ideas we came up with:

1. FIND A REPUTABLE REPAIR SHOP

Because I don't know much about the inner workings of cars (nor do I really want to), a trustworthy car repairman is just about as important as a good hairdresser in my mind. They make hard to understand concepts easier to grasp, and won't convince you that a very expensive part needs to be replaced, when clearly, you can get a few thousand more miles out of it.

Thankfully, we've been lucky enough to find one we trust. It's a little bit of a drive, but our confidence in his abilities makes it worth the service and the price. Ask around to see who friends and family trust, or carefully read through reviews on Yelp.com. You want someone who cares about your car as much as, if not more than, you do!

2. PERFORM PREVENTATIVE MAINTENANCE

Regularly scheduled tune-ups like oil changes, tire pressure checks, tire rotation, and brake checks will make your car last much longer. You don't have to go crazy with these, as sometimes shops like to get you in the door and upsell you on excessive maintenance packages (see point #1). But you *should* check your car manual for each manufacturer's recommended maintenance schedule, just to be safe.

These items help prevent bigger and more expensive issues from happening down the road and are non-negotiable if you want a car that lasts. For example, if you don't change the oil often enough, your engine could seize up and not work at all. At that point, you have to make the decision to either replace the engine or get a new car—they're *that* expensive!

Sometimes it's hard to remember exactly when to do these regularly scheduled tune-ups (or even know what's included). To download a Car Maintenance Checklist with all the recommended to-dos, be sure to visit

CreativeSavingsBlog.com/ExpenseResources

A few things listed on there are best left to a professional, but many can be done yourself for a fraction of the price.

READER TIP:

There are plenty of repairs novices can do with basic tools. Changing your alternator and fan belts is relatively easy. I saved $100 easily by replacing my own alternator, and it's only secured on the motor with a few bolts. Changing your own oil, transmission fluid, and performing a radiator flush are all things that can be done by following videos on YouTube.

—Derrick, MI

3. USE COUPONS

I don't know about you, but I constantly receive coupons in the mail from our car manufacturer and several local repair shops. These coupons always offer major discounts on oil changes, tire rotations, brake checks, and other similar tune-up jobs, and range anywhere from 15-40% off!

If you're not loyal to any one shop, or haven't found a trustworthy car mechanic yet, you may want to take advantage of these coupons and try a few places before deciding on the one you like most. Don't forget to check Groupon.com for any specials they might be running as well.

4. KNOW YOUR PRICES

Regardless of who your mechanic is, research the repair in question before settling on a price. RepairPal.com allows you to find the average price of a repair in your area so you know for sure you're not being duped, and can get a general idea of what things cost before spending any money.

Depending on the repair in question, you may be able to shop around for parts, watch a YouTube tutorial on how to install them, and save a little money on the final bill. Or, you could just pay your mechanic the labor it takes for him to do it at his shop. We were able to buy tires much cheaper online than from the garage, and our mechanic didn't mind at all.

Craigslist, Ebay, or JustParts.com will be your go-to sites for cheaper prices on things like side mirrors, windshield wiper motors, and more, but don't be afraid to do a little Googling too.

READER TIP:

Try calling places like Pick n' Pull or other auto wrecking yards. They keep an inventory of parts and you can save a ton by going there because the parts aren't brand new!

—Lindsey, WA

5. CONSIDER BECOMING A ONE-CAR FAMILY

Never in a million years could I have imagined we would become a one-car family. Now that I work from home, I do admit it's easier to survive with just one vehicle, but it wasn't impossible when we both held down outside jobs and were forced to make it work. It took a little more coordination with both our schedules, but it was one less piece of expensive equipment to worry about.

If you're tired of paying for repairs, upkeep, and extra insurance for an additional car, give this some serious consideration. We have spent far less with one vehicle than we did two, and I haven't regretted our decision since!

6. DON'T FORGET INCIDENTALS

We've already discussed fuel prices in Day 6, and we'll tackle car insurance in Day 8, but there are other costs to consider too, such as tolls and parking fees. While seemingly insignificant at first glance, they can quickly grow into unmanageable expenses if you're not careful.

To Save on Tolls:

- Choose an alternate route, if it doesn't take you too much out of the way

- Buy an annual pass (if offered) to save money on a frequent route

To Save on Parking:

- Park farther away in an economy lot and catch a bus, or walk
- Pay by the month (usually less than if you pay daily)
- Switch lots depending on the time of day or on weekends when prices are higher

Both of these items, depending on how often you encounter them, need to be budgeted for right along with your occasional maintenance and repair fees so they don't catch you by surprise.

The purchase of a car is just the beginning...it's the cost of ownership that follows you for as long as you have the vehicle. Personally, I think it's smart (or nerdy, depends on who you ask) to track how much you spend on your car over the years. We have a Car Maintenance and Repair Log and write down any time we change the tires, buy new brakes, or take it in for an oil change. It also helps me know which of our cars were duds, and which brands we will be purchasing again.

If you'd like to download your own Car Maintenance and Repair Log (I highly recommend it!), you can do so at

CreativeSavingsBlog.com/ExpenseResources

DAY 7 ACTION PLAN

- Download a Preventative Maintenance Schedule to keep your car running smoothly and avoid potential issues down the road.

- Budget a little bit extra so you're not caught by surprise when repairs, or even smaller incidentals like parking fees, happen.

- Print out and use a Car Maintenance and Repair log to keep track of how much you spend on your car, for what, and when.

Day 8:
REDUCE CAR INSURANCE RATES

If you consider yourself a safe driver, paying enormously high insurance rates is almost offensive. Years of no accidents, no tickets, and no major catastrophes should count for something, right? But instead, you're rewarded with a policy that creeps higher and higher every year. One tiny fender-bender and your premium could jump from manageable to sky-high in a matter of days, and that's a lot of pressure when you're out on the road.

Thankfully, I haven't experienced any accidents besides the occasional tap, but I never expected our home in Upstate NY to flood, let alone drown my little red car "safely" parked in the driveway. After declaring our car a total loss, our insurance company gave us a very generous check to buy a new one, and I'm pretty sure we got our money's worth in premiums that year! Hondas do a great job of retaining their value, FYI.

While I wish we didn't have to experience losing a car, not to mention all the paperwork involved to file a claim and buy a new one, this is the perfect example of never knowing what *could* happen. Insurance companies bank on these what if's to figure out what to charge, and that's why it's vital to have good coverage despite the fact that you might not ever use it.

When it comes to shopping for car insurance, though, let's be honest—it's a huge inconvenience to call around for quotes, compare coverage, and make sure you're working with a company that has your best interest at heart. It's no wonder the minute you sign those final papers they go straight into the filing cabinet never to be seen or referenced again.

But that's when the real work begins. Saving on car insurance doesn't mean you set it up once and forget it. You have to continually review your policy to make sure you're getting the best rate possible. These six tips are the perfect place to start:

1. PAY YOUR PREMIUM IN FULL

One of the easiest ways to save on car insurance is to pay your entire policy in full, which means annual or six-month payments instead of monthly ones. Insurance companies tack on extra fees for monthly payment plans, and you can avoid these entirely just by setting aside enough money each paycheck until your bill is due.

Let me show you a real life example taken from one of my 2013 car insurance bills:

> A six-month policy premium came in the mail saying we owed $633.13 for our next policy term. But if we paid the bill in full, it dropped all the way down to $506.50—**a total savings of $126.63**—just for paying what we should have anyway!

If you don't currently pay your premium in full, this method will take some getting used to before it becomes a habit, but it's more than worth the effort. It's pretty easy to implement too. Just use that number on your annual or six-month bill and divide it by the number of months each term covers.

That's the amount you need to set aside every month in order to pay your premium the next time it arrives!

2. DON'T CARRY EXCESS COVERAGE

If you've never examined your car insurance policy before (it's exciting bedside reading, I know), it's good practice to meticulously comb through your policy and make sure you're not paying for more than you need.

For instance, you could drop rental reimbursement, towing assistance, or even comprehensive coverage to save a little extra money each year. These policies might already be covered by companies like AAA, meaning you potentially double pay for the same service. However, you'll definitely want to speak to a professional before decreasing something like liability coverage. If you were to ever get into an accident with an expensive car, you could be left holding a hefty bill, not to mention an unfortunate lawsuit!

You'll also want to consider the age of your car before making any big decisions, especially regarding comprehensive coverage. If it's newer, you may want to keep this portion. If it's older, and typically valued at less than $1,000, it probably won't be worth the payout.

JUST TO CLARIFY:

> **Comprehensive Coverage:** Insurance that covers your vehicle against damages resulting from incidents other than collision—theft, vandalism, flooding, fire, damage due to a natural disaster, etc.

3. INCREASE YOUR DEDUCTIBLE

Just like we talked about with homeowner's insurance, a higher deductible is one of the best ways to guarantee a lower premium. But it can also be a risky move. If you get into a fender-bender or more serious accident, you're suddenly out hundreds of dollars to take care of whatever damage has occurred. One wrong turn, and your bank account takes a pretty big hit!

I can't harp on this point enough; you *must* have an Emergency Fund in place to cover your deductible in case something like this happens. You should also think long and hard about what you decide to claim. Something miniscule like a small dent or missing headlight might actually be cheaper to pay out of pocket, rather than file a claim and deal with mounds of paperwork—not to mention a potential price hike in your premium because you actually used their service.

If the idea of permanently increasing your deductible scares you, consider this as a temporary solution for a few months. A higher deductible might be just the thing to get you through a financial rough patch, and you can always go back and lower the deductible again, if needed. Just be sure you have that Emergency Fund!

4. TAKE ADVANTAGE OF SPECIAL DISCOUNTS

I can't even begin to tell you how many commercials I see featuring one insurance company after another, each vying for our attention...and our dollars. But that's also a good thing. It means they want our business, and will sometimes give us quite a few discounts to get it!

Each company should have its own list of available discounts on their website, but even if they don't, be assertive and ask exactly what they can give you that other companies can't. Here's a list of the most typical offers:

- Bundling your policies

- Maintaining good credit

- Being part of an association, such as an alumni of a university

- Being employed with a particular company

- Maintaining low mileage

- Installing specific car safety features (car alarms, anti-lock brakes, etc.)

- Maintaining good grades in school

- Enrolling in paperless statements

Depending on what promotions companies are currently running, you could also take advantage of specific driving rewards programs. Just be sure it will truly save you money—some programs offer rewards, but charge a higher rate.

READER TIP:

These tips are approved by an insurance agent—me! I no longer work as an agent, but I did for three years. Sometimes the cash back incentive for no accidents actually raises your rates, so you're paying extra to get your own money back. It's better not to take it in my opinion.

—Jamie, MD

5. TAKE A DEFENSIVE DRIVING COURSE

Every few years, you have the opportunity to enroll in a defensive driving course for a discount of 10-20% off your insurance premium. These courses generally last between four to twelve hours, and are offered through local driving schools, private companies, employee programs, or even on-line through DefensiveDriving.com. A class about safe driving habits might be a really boring way to spend your day, but it also helps save money!

One word of caution—before you sign up for *any* class, call your insurance company and be sure they accept whatever course you're taking. Thankfully, defensive driving classes aren't too expensive (I've seen prices anywhere from $25-$75), but I'd hate for you to pay that money and not have it lower your insurance after all.

6. RESEARCH THE COMPETITION

Gathering quotes from a variety of car insurance companies will give you the leverage you need to negotiate better rates. Take some time to compare prices, and don't forget to include any of the perks or discounts available with that particular company. It might help to create a spreadsheet so you can see everything side by side, but I also say that because I'm slightly obsessed with spreadsheets!

Researching quotes is time-consuming, but practicing our due diligence and comparing information from other companies allowed us to find a six-month policy for $371. This saved us a total of $135.50 from the 2013 bill I mentioned in an earlier example.

Price is an important factor, but also keep an eye on customer satisfaction. And don't be swayed by "limited time offer" conditions. Buying car insurance should be a carefully thought out process that allows you time to consider all alternatives. Walk away and choose someone else if you feel too pressured to commit.

Remember, you are your best advocate and it's your responsibility to stay on top of that rate. Know exactly what you are paying for and carefully review your renewal policy every year. You never know what savings lie ahead!

DAY 8 ACTION PLAN:

- If you haven't already, set aside monthly payments towards your auto insurance so you can pay it in full when the bill arrives.

- Ask about discounts at your current insurance company, and compare rates with others to make sure you're getting the best deal.

- See if you're eligible to sign up for a defensive driving course...then do it.

Part 3:
Reduce Food Expenses

Day 9:
SLASH YOUR GROCERY BILL

Whenever I talk to women and families about saving money, lowering groceries is almost always at the top of the list. Why? Because the majority of them spend hundreds, if not thousands, of dollars on food each month, creating a huge financial strain for already maxed out budgets.

As food prices rise and life gets a little busier every year, we have less time than ever before to scout out the best savings. And if you try to eat healthy or have a specific food allergy, forget it. The sky-high prices of organic fruits and veggies, not to mention anything labeled gluten-free, double and triple your grocery bill, almost like an unlawful punishment for being conscious about what we feed our families.

My grocery budget has experienced its own financial roller coaster from month to month. Some weeks, I do really well with my spending, and others, not so much. I most often go over budget because I stop paying attention to sales and focus instead on getting in and out of the store as quickly as possible. I don't particularly like grocery shopping if you can't tell!

It's not until I pull out the crumpled receipt from my pocket and enter it into my Expense Tracker that I clearly see the results of my laziness. Once again, I've gone over budget, and guilt becomes that old familiar wakeup call. It's time to get back up and try again, no matter how hard or impossible it might be to start over.

The thing is, I know it's more than feasible to cut costs in this area. I've done it, and I'm going to teach you how to do it too. Because even though we have to eat, we don't have to eat expensively. Just a few shopping habits have the potential to drastically reduce your spending, and on the flipside, give you immediate savings. These creative ways to slash your grocery bill make the biggest difference!

1. SHOP YOUR PANTRY

Last year, when our grocery budget was super tight, and I mean *super*, I tried to see what we already had in our pantry to create meals rather than head to the grocery store. I came up with seven (yes, seven!) extra dinners with a simple food inventory and pairing ingredients I already had. It took about twenty to thirty minutes, but helped us delay that grocery trip a little while longer. It was great to use up some of the ingredients I had forgotten about too!

Here's an example of the ingredients I had and what I could make:

- Ground beef + BBQ sauce + ketchup + hamburger buns = Sloppy Joes

- Lettuce + cheese + dressing + croutons = Salads

- Canned soup + bread + cheese = Grilled Cheese Sandwiches and Tomato Soup

- Chicken + cream of chicken soup + cheese + broccoli + bread crumbs = Chicken Casserole

- Chicken + bread crumbs + eggs + seasonings = Popcorn Chicken

- Pasta + cheese = Mac n' Cheese
- Noodles + sauce + cheese + seasonings = Pasta Dish

I encourage you to go through your pantry, fridge, and freezer today and see what meals you can brainstorm based on the ingredients you have. The Shop Your Stock Worksheet will help, and is available at

CreativeSavingsBlog.com/ExpenseResources

2. MAKE BUDGET-FRIENDLY MEALS

Whenever you plan weekly or monthly meals (which saves you time and money), focus on recipes that cost less than $1/ serving. This stretches the food you *do* buy so you don't have to run to the store as often, and can make more meals, for less money.

Don't create meals that require oddball or expensive in-gredients either. It's best to stick to the basics when budgets are tight, and shop seasonally whenever possible. A food specific Pinterest board is a great idea to collect inspiration and try new recipes. You also might want to visit a few of my favorite frugal foodie blogs too:

- BudgetBytes.com
- GoodCheapEats.com
- CheapRecipeBlog.com

If you want a ready-made meal plan that does all the work for you, I highly recommend eMeals. This meal planning ser-vice matches up recipes with grocery store sales and offers over twenty different plans according to tastes and prefer-ences. It does cost a tiny subscription per month, but the budget-friendly plan can cut costs to $85/week for a family of four! Visit CreativeSavingsBlog.com/eMeals to sign up for a free trial.

READER TIP:

Our family is building a greenhouse this fall so we can utilize it immediately starting in the spring! We intend to grow our own things to make veggies— something we don't have to buy.

—*Naomi, PA*

3. EAT LEFTOVERS

I'm not a huge fan of leftovers, but in an effort to eliminate food waste, both Joseph and I have learned to tolerate them a little bit more. One of my tricks is to freeze individual leftovers rather than sticking them in the fridge until they mold. This is particularly helpful if we have something like extra biscuits or soup, because we can just freeze the rest for another busy night.

What do you do when leftovers simply aren't appealing on their own? Turn them into a new recipe, of course!

- If you have leftover meat, make a sandwich the next day, or sprinkle on a salad.
- If you have leftover mashed potatoes, shape into patties and cook in a skillet to make potato pancakes.
- If you have leftover veggies and noodles, make a soup. The possibilities are endless!

Another thing I like to do is warm up leftovers on the stove or in a convection oven. It seems to revive refrigerated food a lot better than the microwave.

4. SHOP DISCOUNT FOOD STORES

Discount grocery stores, such as Aldi or Save-A-Lot offer brands that are priced much lower than products sold at regular grocers. Try switching over most of your shopping to one of these stores, and you'll see a big difference in your budget. Not every brand is over-the-top amazing, so you'll want to do some trial and error before you get a hang of what's good and what's not.

Be sure to visit a discounted bread store too if you're lucky enough to have one in your area. These stores sell bread products that expire in a day or so, but bread always freezes well. Use this as your golden opportunity to stock up and save!

Lastly, there are scratch and dent stores available with discounted and "damaged" goods similar to what you would find at a furniture outlet. These stores offer products at a fraction of the price, and rarely have anything wrong with them besides mismatched labels and an actual dent or two. The blog *A Mom's Paradise* has a pretty comprehensive list of scratch and dent stores by state, which you can access at

CreativeSavingsBlog.com/Dent

READER TIP:

Over the last five years, we have reduced our grocery budget to $300 a month for a family of four. It is definitely a challenge as food prices continue to increase. Learning to view meat as an add-in or side instead of a main course has been the biggest help. That, and cutting out most prepared or pre-packaged foods and cooking them from scratch.

—Lisa, TX

5. SHOP IN BULK

There's some debate on whether warehouse club memberships (think Sam's, BJ's, or Costco) are actually worth it, but I believe they are. However, just like anything else you spend money on, you have to be smart when shopping these kinds of stores.

Start by checking each store's prices before making a final commitment. Find a friend or family member with a card, and write down the prices of your favorite items, as well as the unit cost, to determine whether or not each item is indeed cheaper than your regular or discount grocery store. You may also want to consider going in with a friend to share the yearly cost.

It is also important to remember expiration dates. Bulk foods are fantastic for pantry items that last for months, but beware of refrigerated items that can't be frozen. You don't want to trade savings for food waste!

6. USE COUPONS

I am definitely *not* an extreme couponer—sometimes I will go weeks without clipping a single piece of paper. However, when I do take the time to put together a strategic shopping list and match it up with store sales and coupons, I notice a pretty big difference in my grocery bill for weeks to come.

Couponing could be a book in itself (there's *that* much to talk about!), but the main things to remember are:

- Make coupons last, not first. Figure out what you need to buy, then print and clip coupons based on items you know you'll use. I list my favorite printable coupon sites at

CreativeSavingsBlog.com/Coupons

- Stack store coupons and manufacturer coupons with store sales for the biggest savings. Many stores will even accept competitors' coupons!

- Be organized. Make a grocery list based on your meal plan and store sales flyers, then write down any coupons you have next to each item. This saves time because you know exactly what coupons you have for what.

- Keep an accordion file (or binder) for your coupons and make sure they are always updated and accessible.

Another thing you can do is track store sales and stock up when prices are ultra low. Bonus if you can use a coupon too! Most items go on sale every six to eight weeks, so buy enough to last until the next sales cycle. It might sound counterintuitive to spend more upfront, but you'll save more in the long run.

READER TIP:

I am lazy when it comes to clipping coupons from the paper, but I love Target! I use TotallyTarget.com to help me save the most. I use Cartwheel on my phone and print Target coupons before I go and try to match things up. I also use smartphone apps like Ibotta, Checkout51, Jingit, and Snap by Groupon to get $20 back a month. I also just started using Walmart's Savings Catcher and I've made back $3 in two trips. Not a lot, but it's adding up fast!

—Krystal, SunnySweetDays.com

When it comes right down to it, saving on groceries completely depends on the price you pay. I would encourage you to start a price book (if you haven't already) and keep track of what your basic, and favorite, foods cost. This helps you know exactly when to stock up so you always score that rock-bottom price.

Many grocery shoppers write down their prices in a simple purse-sized notebook, but I prefer to keep track of mine on Google Drive so I can access it on my phone and update price points with ease.

DAY 9 ACTION PLAN:

- If you don't know how much money you're currently spending on groceries, do some math to come up with a final total. Then commit to trying one of the above methods and lower that amount by $25/month to start.

- Go through your pantry, fridge, and freezer and come up with seven meals you can make without going to the store. Use the Shop Your Stock Worksheet to help.

- Track prices and write them down in your own price book. Try to pay attention to sales cycles and any available coupons too!

Day 10:
EAT OUT FOR LESS

My number one spending downfall (besides buying more books than I could possibly read in a lifetime) is eating out at local restaurants and fast food chains. There are many days when I simply don't feel like cooking, or have time to cook, and the easiest solution is to let someone else do it for me.

Especially on Sundays.

There's nothing more satisfying than stepping outside those church doors, knowing that you don't have to fix the noon meal. The hardest part is actually deciding *where* to go!

But I'd be blind if I didn't notice that restaurants (even fast food ones) have jumped in price over the past few years. $10-$15 for a simple meal, $4-$5 for an ice cream cone—it's getting insane. It's simply not practical to sacrifice your entire food budget for the sake of convenience, not when you can eat at home for much less. Plus, if you have a big family, eating out gets even more expensive. It's not like restaurant-grade meals are always the healthiest food to eat either.

While I would hate to give up our love for restaurants indefinitely (because I think they can be enjoyed in moderation), there are some really smart ways to make eating at home more enjoyable, and eating out practically a steal. Try these six ideas the next time you want to head out on the town without the guilt!

1. MAKE MEALS YOU ACTUALLY LIKE

Many times, my reason for eating out is simply that I don't like any of the meals we've been making at home. Either that, or they've become too boring.

Switch up your meal plan and try some new and exciting dishes that help you enjoy being in the kitchen again, or experiment with a few of your favorite restaurant meals at home using a copycat recipe. I recommend you start a Pinterest board specifically for this purpose. There are hundreds of recipes on Pinterest to try!

When you settle on ten to fifteen meals that the whole family enjoys, keep them written down on a Family Favorites Worksheet to reference every time you write up a meal plan. You can download the worksheet at

CreativeSavingsBlog.com/ExpenseResources

2. DON'T LEAVE WITHOUT A COUPON

One of our personal eating out "rules" is that when we *do* set aside money for a special night out, we have to use a coupon. If you're like me and never remember to take your printed coupons, pull up the coupon on your phone and show it to the waiter or cashier. They almost always accept it, and you don't have to worry about forgetting a coupon ever again.

In regards to where to find coupons:

- **Subscribe to Restaurant Mailing Lists –** I subscribe to a ton of email lists, so I almost always have a wide range of weekly coupons to choose from. I would encourage you to start a second email address specifically for this purpose, but I also use Unroll.me to "roll up" all my subscriptions into one email to limit the endless supply of notifications.

- **Sign Up for Birthday Freebies** – Many restaurants offer free food on your birthday, and usually include your entire birthday month as a valid time period to use it. That means you could eat for free all month long, and at a variety of restaurants! For the most up-to-date list of Birthday Freebies, visit

  CreativeSavingsBlog.com/Birthday

- **Buy a City Savings Book** – For $20-$30, you can purchase a paperback book filled with local deals and coupons. It's easy to stash this book away and forget about it, so keep it within eyesight! Even better if it's accessible within your car to use whenever you go out.

- **Save Your Receipt** – The next time you throw a receipt away, take a second look—there might be a coupon on it! Many restaurants reward you for taking a two-minute survey on their website or over the phone, and will offer a free food item or 15% off your next meal in return.

- **Check Groupon.com** – Groupon is a great place to find a deal on local restaurants, and gives you the opportunity to try new dives for less. You never know what hidden gem you might find in your neighborhood!

READER TIP:

This year, I purchased an Attractions Dining and Value Guide (attractionsbook.com) for our area (think the entertainment books schools sell) for $25. We've already made our money back and we've only had it 1.5 months. I've given coupons to some coworkers and parents as well, so I'm spreading the joy too!

—Kim, VA

3. ORDER WATER

Joseph used to work in the restaurant industry, and I was shocked when he told me what kind of profit margin eating establishments make on drinks, especially soda. What costs essentially pennies for syrup and carbonation translates into $2-$4 per person on your bill, not including refills!

Water is such an easy replacement and doesn't cost a thing. You are better off health-wise too.

Ask for lemon or lime wedges to give it a bit of flavor, or bring your own powder packets to quickly turn it into lemonade if you can't stand the plain taste.

The key is to make sodas a rare, but special treat. It will be hard at first, but this simple switch literally pays you dollars in savings. And if you can't give up soda just yet, try splitting a large drink with your family. Just be careful—most establishments frown on getting free refills if you share drinks among family members, as refills should be per person only.

4. SPLIT A MEAL

Food portions these days are HUGE. I usually cut my entree in half immediately after receiving it, then take leftovers home for tomorrow's lunch. I've also thrown in a few extra rolls that were left over from the dinner table too, but that might be a result of my carb addiction. Either way, I figure if I'm spending that kind of money on food, I better savor each bite and make it last!

Also consider splitting a meal between two, even three people to get more mileage out of the final bill. If an entree doesn't look big enough, you may want to order an appetizer as well to be sure you have enough. These are often less expensive than regular dinners, and fill your stomach before the main course.

For fast food chains, order a big carton of fries and share among family members for even more savings. It's much cheaper than individual packs, and lets parents determine their kids' serving sizes beforehand.

READER TIP:

From the very beginning, our daughter eats what we eat (aside from baby food). We do not buy kids' meals at restaurants. She's only 2.5 so she never eats more than a few bites anyway; she just shares whatever I'm eating. That saves at least $5 every time!

—*Jennifer, MI*

5. EAT WHERE KIDS EAT FREE

It's pretty crazy how many restaurants offer "kids eat free" days. MyKidsEatFree.com is the best website to find up-to-date promotions in your area, but I would still call ahead to make sure they haven't discontinued the program.

You can also Google "where do kids eat free in [INSERT CLOSEST METRO AREA]" for a few different results. Read the fine print, though, as many of these hinge on a paying adult for each cheap, or free, kid's meal.

While other restaurants might not have a "kids eat free" offer, they do advertise discounts and kid-only specials. And when you have a family, no matter the size, it's no secret that eating out costs add up quickly. Take advantage of any kid-friendly opportunity available to give your wallet a break!

6. COLLECT OR REQUEST GIFT CARDS

It never hurts to ask for gift cards to favorite restaurants for Christmas, birthdays, and even Mother's Day gifts. I know I certainly don't mind! Who needs more clutter anyway, when you can take your family out for a yummy meal and experience togetherness instead? Just be sure to keep your gift cards organized so you don't forget to use them.

You can also buy gift cards for yourself during holiday promos. Every year around Christmastime, restaurants promote specials like, "Buy a $25 gift card, get an extra $5 free." Restaurant.com is another place that offers local discounts up to 80% off.

I'll admit, it's always nice to go out to eat on someone else's dime, but it comes with an extra responsibility in regards to tipping. Be sure to tip on the full amount of your meals, not the remaining balance on the restaurant receipt. It's the right thing to do for our hardworking waiters and waitresses!

Maybe you're already disciplined in this area and hardly eat out at all. Good for you! You'll want to read the previous chapter on how to slash your grocery bill, but for the rest of us, I have a different challenge:

See if you can go thirty days without grabbing takeout and instead, focus on making meals at home. You can even schedule in some friend and family visits to take the pressure off creating all those meals—just don't tell them that's why you're doing it!

Anyone can do anything for thirty days, and this habit gives you the willpower you need to say no. Not to mention the potential hundreds of dollars you can save at the end of the month, which is an awesome perk in itself.

DAY 10 ACTION PLAN:

- Form a personal or family "rule" that you only eat out with a coupon, and save the "withouts" for special occasions.

- Try something you don't normally do the next time you go out. Order water instead of soda, or split a drink—even a meal. Take home leftovers, then make sure to eat them.

- Start an eating out spending freeze for the next thirty days, and focus instead on creating simple meals at home.

Part 4: Reduce Utility Expenses

Day 11:
CUT YOUR WATER BILL

Water bills are one of my least favorite expenses to budget for, mostly because they change so often, but more so because they're super hard to control. The more you use, the more expensive your bill, and it changes based on how long you shower, brush your teeth, wash your hands, or even water your plants! Not to mention that when out of town guests come to visit, your bill can double in a matter of weeks.

We were thrilled to find out that our home in Florida was on a well system, but the city has plans to switch us over to city water some time in the next ten years, and we know we'll have to be more conscious about water usage then. We're hoping it's longer, but until that time comes, it doesn't hurt to practice a few water conserving habits now!

Despite our lucking out down South, we're still not completely exempt from water bills. Our rental back North sends us a pretty hefty statement every quarter in light of the two families that currently live there, making it a painful pill to swallow, and pay, for sure. Especially when we're not the ones controlling usage anymore.

But that's what it really boils down to anyway, right? Using less water. Although we can't predict exactly how much our water bills will be, we can still make a significant impact based on how much we actually use. Sure, you can try to stop water leaks, upgrade to high-efficiency appliances, and even turn crunchy enough to build a rain barrel (which are all good things by the way), but you could still end up with a sky-high water bill simply because you use *too much*.

Smart, daily water habits are where the true savings lie, and these first few steps are where you need to start if you want to get that water bill under control again.

1. BE SMART IN THE SHOWER

I'll be honest—I love a nice long relaxing shower, but when you really stop to think about it, it's crazy how much water you waste for the sake of a spa-like experience. Try to shorten the length of your showers, and/or turn the water off to suds up with shampoo, conditioner, and body wash. And if you always shave in the shower, try filling the sink with warm water and shave from there instead.

Something else you shouldn't overlook is the age and efficiency of your showerhead. A conventional showerhead actually pours out three to five gallons *per minute*, while a more efficient low-flow head only uses two. If you take a fifteen to twenty minute shower, this means you could save fifteen to sixty gallons, just by changing your showerhead!

Here's a real life example:

> When I crunched the numbers of our latest water bill from New York, we pay an approximate $.0112 per gallon of water, so just over a penny. For a 15-minute shower using 5 gallons per minute, that one shower costs $.84 for just one person.

> However, if you switch to a low-flow showerhead and take a 15-minute shower using 2 gallons per

minute, that one shower costs $.34 for just one person—a $.50 difference.

That might not sound like much, but let's say that one person takes a shower every single day for a year. You pay only $124.10 for that shower as opposed to $306.60—a **$182.50 difference for one person!** Think about how much you could save with a family of four, or if you could cut that shower down to 10 minutes, let alone 5.[5]

For those of you who love lounging in the tub, try to limit this as only a special treat, or don't fill the tub all the way. Half is plenty to enjoy a relaxing soak, and even less can be used for splashing kiddos.

READER TIP:

My two youngest bathe together, and for my older two I bought a timer from Dollar Tree to set for seven minutes for their showers. When it goes off they have to get out. Amazingly it only took a short while for them to be trained. They don't need the timers anymore; they wash and get out when they need to.

—*Jessica, CT*

2. DO LESS LAUNDRY

I don't know about you, but we easily get into the habit of wearing clothes or using towels only once, then immediately throwing them in the hamper to wash. But when we consciously take the time to go through each piece to see if we can indeed wear it (or use it) again, we find that almost half of that pile doesn't need to be laundered at all. More laundry = more water usage, and less laundry = more savings!

The other key is to wash laundry at the most optimal settings, meaning don't do extra large loads when you only have a few items to launder. Make sure every load is full, or adjust water levels accordingly. Laundering most clothing items in cold water is a good habit to get into as well. It might not save on water usage, but it *will* save on the electricity or gas used to heat your water.

3. PRACTICE DAILY HABITS

Besides shorter showers, and wearing clothes more than once, here are a few more daily habits that help reduce water usage:

- Use one drinking glass per day to cut down on the amount you have to wash.
- Keep a pitcher of water in the fridge to use, rather than let it "run" until cold.
- Water plants in the morning to create less evaporation.
- Don't run the dishwasher unless it's fully loaded.
- Turn off the water while you brush your teeth.
- Turn off the water in between hand washing dishes, or use tubs to rinse instead.
- Depending on how brave you are, you could also possibly skip a few toilet flushes!

While it might be hard to remember these seven things every day, choose just one or two to focus on until you're doing them automatically. Then move on to create one or two more habits until they become second nature.

4. KEEP AN EYE OUT FOR LEAKS

A couple years ago, we had a slightly leaky toilet that resulted in a $320 water bill...for the *month*. How did we not know our toilet was leaking? Because the tank didn't have a good seal, and as a result, went unnoticed for quite a while. Oh my, did it result in a crazy expensive bill!

As you can probably imagine, we watch our toilets, sinks, and under-counter plumbing pipes like a hawk now. It's a good reminder to check for leaks every now and then, even ones you assume might not be much of a problem. A slow, steady drip produces approximately 100 drips per minute, resulting in 330 gallons per month.

Some leaks are fixable with a few basic tools and a couple YouTube tutorials, but others might require the assistance of a plumber. Depending on the significance of the leak, it could be costly, but rest assured, this will pay for itself over the course of the year.

DID YOU KNOW?

Washing dishes by hand actually uses more water than the dishwasher. Stop over-rinsing dishes and let your dishwasher do the work instead.

5. UPDATE YOUR APPLIANCES

I know it might seem counterintuitive to pay more to save more, but at some point, you should save up to replace all your inefficient appliances with energy saving ones. This includes items like your dishwasher, toilet, and washing machine.

Energy efficient appliances are made to reduce the amount of water flow, thus decreasing your quarterly bill. For instance, a low-flow toilet uses as little as 1.6 gallons to flush, as opposed to the five to seven for conventional models. A dishwasher installed before 1994 wastes more than ten gallons per cycle, while an Energy Star appliance could save over 1,600 gallons over its lifetime. An older washing machine uses 23 gallons of water per load, compared to the thirteen gallons used by an energy efficient one.

If you can afford it, energy saving appliances are the way to go, and most allow you to claim a tax credit at the end of the year too. To find out more about what characteristics to look for in an energy efficient product, or which products will give you that tax credit, visit EnergyStar.gov.

6. MAKE A RAIN BARREL

One of the projects on our home wish list is a DIY rain barrel. We have strict watering laws here in Florida, and I know it would eliminate so much waste since it rains almost every single day!

If you're not familiar with what a rain barrel does, this tool collects water from rainstorms that can then be used to water your grass, garden, or houseplants without hooking into your main water system. It's essentially free water—nature gives it right to you.

Buying a rain barrel is certainly an option, but it's much cheaper to craft one yourself out of a garbage can and attach it to a rain gutter. Search "DIY rain barrel" on Pinterest, and you'll find a ton of tutorials to make your own.

I wouldn't consider any of these saving options drastic measures to cut down your water bill right away, but they do add up over time. Just a few tips practiced consistently can make a big difference on your bottom line, and that's not just good for the wallet, it's good for the environment too!

DAY 11 ACTION PLAN

- Time yourself in the shower and try to cut that time by a few minutes every day.

- Choose one smart, daily water habit to implement this week.

- Start a separate savings account to save up for a high-grade energy efficient appliance, if needed.

Day 12:
LOWER YOUR ELECTRIC BILL

Do you ever take electricity for granted? I know I certainly do. It only takes one of our infamous Florida thunderstorms for me to remember just how much I rely on power throughout the day.

But this lifestyle of convenience also brings a greater dependence on more gadgets, more technology, and more outlets to plug everything into...which isn't bad per se, but can result in a pretty hefty electric bill. And if you live in a colder climate during the winter months, you know firsthand the considerable cost difference between January and June!

I honestly thought our electric bill would go down after we moved to Florida, but to my surprise, air conditioning is not cheap. That, and it's kind of necessary. Going without can be downright unbearable during the hot summer months, not to mention the mold and mildew potential from high humidity.

But even though we find ourselves using more electricity as a result of our air conditioner, there are still many other areas besides heating and cooling where we can cut back. There's our refrigerator, washer, dryer, cooking appliances, dishwasher, electronics, and of course, the lamps, ceiling fans, and overhead lights we use every day. When you really stop and think about it, just about everything we own runs on some sort of electricity, so it's no wonder we've become such an energy hungry culture.

While I do agree it's a huge inconvenience to constantly monitor electricity usage, this *is* an area of our budget where we have complete control. Here are six energy saving strategies to implement right away:

1. ADJUST THE TEMPERATURE OF YOUR HOME

Whether you use heat, air conditioning, or both, adjusting your thermostat every time you leave the house or head to bed makes a pretty big difference in your overall bill. The Energy Information Administration (EIA.gov) found that 42% of home energy costs go to heating and cooling, so it's essential to get this part under control!

You can adjust the temperature manually, or buy a programmable thermostat to do all the adjusting for you. Be careful that you don't micromanage too much, though. Constantly changing the temperature wastes more energy than it saves. Here are the two areas I would focus on if you want to see significant savings:

- **In the Winter:** Keep your house at 68° while you're awake and at home, and lower while you're asleep or away.

- **In the Summer:** If you have air conditioning, keep your house at 78° while you're awake and at home, and higher while you're away. You may want to keep the temperature at 78° or lower while you're asleep, as trying to go to bed in a very hot house makes for an uncomfortable situation!

Note: Those who live in hotter climates without much change in season (like Florida) will need to adjust their temperature accordingly.

During the fall and winter months, you may also want to turn off the heat completely, and try using space heaters in areas of the home where you spend the most time. We do this quite often in the winter so our air conditioning system doesn't have to constantly shift between heating and cooling, wasting more energy. Don't be afraid to shut off other parts of your home either. Rooms that don't get much use should be closed off so they don't take extra heat to warm them up, or air to cool them down.

2. CHECK YOUR WINDOWS AND DOORS FOR LEAKS

In the past, we have both rented and owned 100-year-old houses in NY that made it quite difficult to be energy efficient. Nothing makes your furnace or air conditioner work overtime like having a drafty window that lets out all your energy!

Even though it didn't look very pretty, we always bought plastic insulator kits (available at home improvement stores) and placed them over our windows to keep the heat in. We also stuffed cracks with rags and blankets whenever possible. Although it was a little embarrassing when we had company over, it helped a lot.

Some other things you can do to minimize leaks:

- Use heavy curtains and/or blinds over windows. These keep the house warm in the winter, and cool in the summer.

- Place foam insulation pads behind electrical outlets and switches. These cost less than $2 and plug holes you may not have otherwise thought about.

- Use strips of insulation around doors and windows.

You may also want to consider better insulation in your attic and crawl spaces. Heat rises and the more you can keep it from leaving through your roof, the better. We invested in this a few years ago, and even though it was more expensive than we wanted, it did make a huge difference in future bills.

3. UNPLUG APPLIANCES AND OTHER DEVICES

Take a minute to look around your house...is your toaster oven plugged in? What about lamps? Maybe a phone charger...or two? It takes just a few minutes to plug and unplug these items, and though one appliance might not make that big of a difference, a handful of them do.

DID YOU KNOW?

After heating and cooling, dehumidifiers are one of the biggest electricity and energy hogs.[6]

Make it a habit to unplug your kitchen appliances when not in use, and put away your chargers when you don't need them. If you have a bunch of cords in the same general area, grab a surge protector that you can easily switch on and off.

It does take some getting used to, but every little bit helps. It's kind of funny, but I always know I've gone on an electricity saving binge when my bagel never toasts the first time around. I always forget to plug the toaster oven back in!

4. CONSERVE LIGHT USAGE

While it seems like a no-brainer to turn lights off when you leave the room, we have all been guilty of forgetting to do this at some point. A simple flick of the switch is all it takes, and you should do this even if you're leaving the room for only a few minutes. Also, table or floor lamps use a lot less energy than overhead lights do, so if you're sitting in a corner reading or watching TV, opt for a smaller lamp to light up the room.

Another option is to switch out all incandescent bulbs after they burn out with CFL bulbs. These work at partial capacity, which means they use 75% less energy, and last ten times longer than normal bulbs. Even though CFL's are more expensive than incandescent bulbs, their long life span makes the switch more than worth it. However, since these bulbs contain mercury, you want to be super careful when disposing of them.

Here's what to do when a CFL bulb breaks[7]:

- Have family and pets leave the room, then air out for about ten to fifteen minutes.
- Shut off the heating or cooling system.
- Scoop up glass with cardboard or paper, and use sticky tape to pick up small fragments.
- Place remnants in a sealable plastic bag and take outdoors to a trash receptacle. Do not leave indoors.

Dimmer switches make a slight difference in energy usage as well. An expert from Florida Power & Light Company (FPL) says dimmer switches extend the life of any bulb, especially if they're a newer model.[8] Dimmable CFL's can save even more, but make sure the package says dimmable before trying it. Many CFL's are surprisingly not.

READER TIP:

Keep the fridge/freezer full so that they don't work as hard. If they're full, the frozen items keep each other and the freezer cold. We also have an extra fridge in our basement so even if we aren't using it for loads of food, we fill it with water bottles.

—*Jennifer, MI*

5. PRACTICE EFFICIENT HOUSEHOLD HACKS

For even more energy savings in your home, here are a few daily habits you should try to practice every single day:

- Set your hot water heater to 120° or below.
- Only let your dishwasher run when it's completely full, and skip the dry cycle. Open up to let dishes air dry.
- Change the air conditioner filter every thirty days so it doesn't have to work as hard.
- Wash a full load of laundry, and wash in cold water whenever possible.
- Hang dry your clothes on a drying rack or clothesline.
- Defrost your freezer twice a year so it doesn't have to work as hard.
- Use the microwave or toaster oven instead of turning on the big oven.

Similar to the habits we mentioned in the chapter about saving on your water bill, it might be hard to remember to do all of these every day. Pick one or two to focus on until they become habit, then move on to practicing all the others on this list.

No matter how diligent you are at reducing electricity usage, if you have outdated, energy hungry appliances, you'll just be fighting a losing battle. If you can't afford to replace any appliances with high efficiency ones right now, start a separate savings account so you have enough to buy one in the future.

Many states offer tax-free shopping days throughout the year, so check to see when Energy Star appliances make that list!

DAY 12 ACTION PLAN:

- Invest in a programmable thermostat or develop the habit of adjusting your temperature while you're asleep or away.

- Take a look around your home and get into the habit of unplugging electronics and appliances when not in use—think of your toaster oven, phone chargers, computers, etc.

- Choose one efficient household hack to implement this week.

Day 13:
TRIM YOUR CABLE BILL

Although I wouldn't go so far as to label myself a TV addict, binge watching a dramatic series is definitely one of my favorite ways to wind down at night. It gives me a chance to leave all the stress of work behind, and get wrapped up in another character's sometimes dysfunctional lifestyle. Seriously, what's not to love about that?

In NY, the perks of Joseph's cable TV job gave us access to every single channel for FREE—and wow, did I take that for granted! Reality hit when we moved to Florida and decided not to get cable right away. We thought it smart to let our finances settle down a bit with the relocation and new job, and bought a digital receiver to grab a few local channels.

Well, three years later we still don't have cable. Sure, I miss the convenience of accessing certain channels, but the boost to our budget is something I haven't regretted since. Plus, the plethora of streaming options gives us the ability to watch our favorite shows *without* the $100 monthly bill.

In fact, a market research company called the NPD Group did a study and found the average cable bill for Americans was $123 in 2015.[9] Crazy, right? That's over $1,400 in the course of a year!

Even though TV is seen as more of a daily staple rather than an occasional luxury, I don't currently see cable providers backing down on their prices. And over the next few years, I can only imagine how many new services will pop up to take advantage of this financial opportunity. But that's also a good thing. More competition has the ability to drive prices down, and ensures the possibility of reducing this monthly expense from a hundred dollar one, to $25 or less.

So whether you're ready to ditch cable altogether and explore a few alternative options, or just want ways to cut back on your monthly bill, all of these ideas will easily lower the amount you spend on television. And yes, they are perfectly legal too!

1. NEGOTIATE WITH YOUR PROVIDER

A very nice phone call to your cable or satellite company is always a great place to start if you don't want to get rid of cable just yet, but still need to lower the monthly cost. These companies are always running promotions to gain new customers, and depending on what the competition offers, you have some serious leverage to negotiate.

If your current provider says no to your very convincing plea, don't take that as the final word. Call back on another day (the representative might be taking out her bad day on you), and if that doesn't work, request a manager or supervisor to look over your account. They usually have the power to give discounts anyway.

Sometimes that oh-so-nice negotiation phone call doesn't go as planned, but that doesn't mean you're stuck. Even though it's inconvenient, you can always switch to another company to try out their service at a promotional rate. Be sure to read the fine print, though, as sometimes these companies require a year or two commitment, and the discount price you signed up under might drop off in the middle of your contract.

2. SCALE BACK TO THE BASICS

Some cable packages advertise over 180 channels, but really, who needs *that* many? I agree, it's nice to relax in front of the TV and surf between various shows and movies after a hard day at work, but if cable is currently a financial strain, you need to consider cutting back.

READER TIP:

One of our favorite resources is our local library, which we use almost every week anyway—you can request any movie from the database online and have it sent to your library if it's not already there.

—*Karla, AK*

Here are a few options:

- Subscribe to only the most basic channels, at least for a few months until you get your finances back on track. Who knows, you might find you don't miss those extras too much after all!

- Get rid of your DVR. If you're renting a DVR from the cable or satellite company, think about buying one of your own (the cost will pay for itself over time), or get rid of it entirely.

- Supplement with TV network apps and internet access. Many popular channels (NBC, CBS, FOX, PBS, The CW, etc.) offer series episodes for free on their respective websites or apps, usually the day after they air. *The catch?* They often limit their selection to only show the last few episodes. This is really useful though if you only watch a few shows and actively keep up after each release.

- Catch up on past seasons from the library. They might not have every TV show available, but you might find a new favorite while browsing the selection!

- Buy an episode or season pass from iTunes or Amazon. At $1.99-$2.99 per episode this has the potential to be expensive, but for a one-time thing, it could be cheaper than paying for cable.

- Buy an antenna to view local, over-the-air channels. Antennas usually cost somewhere between $25-$40, and you can find out which one you should buy, as well as what channels are available to access on AntennaWeb.org. Also, if you live in an urban area and own a Smart TV, an antenna may already be built into your device.

3. SUBSCRIBE TO A STREAMING SERVICE

Alternative programs such as Netflix, Hulu, Amazon, and Sling TV, combined with a streaming device, allow you to watch all of your favorite shows without a huge cable package. Each program requires its own subscription fee, as well as gear to connect it to your TV, but the cost is so minor compared to the average cable bill that it's worth exploring.

Here's a quick breakdown of these services and what they offer:

- **Netflix** trumps the competition when it comes to original content, movies, kid-friendly TV, and ad-free episodes. However, even though they have an extensive library of past seasons, they usually don't air episodes until the entire season is complete. Kind of a pain if you want to keep up with your favorite shows. That said, the movie selection is top-notch.

- **Hulu** is similar to Netflix in that they both stream TV shows and many movies. However, while Netflix waits until a season is over before airing, Hulu features shows the day after they go live. Most past seasons are available in the archives, but occasionally a channel (e.g., The CW) will have a separate contract and give them access only to the last five episodes. The only downside is the basic Hulu version features a few commercials, but they also offer an ad-free subscription for just a few dollars more per month.

- **Amazon Prime** isn't just for two-day shipping; this service also features hundreds of movies and shows that you can watch for free online with your subscription. From my experience with Prime, I didn't find the selection to be awesome for adults, but they do have a lot of kid-friendly movies and shows.

- **Sling TV** is the newbie on the cable alternative market, and so far, I'd say it's a winner. Sling streams through Dish Network, and carries live channels such as HGTV, ESPN, Food Network, Travel, DIY Network and more. Not only can you stream live, but you can also go back and start the current episode over, or watch any episode on that channel within the last 24 hours!

It's best to choose from the above services based on your personal preferences. If you have kids, you might want to go with Amazon Prime. If you're a movie junkie, Netflix is probably your cup of tea. Love to binge watch TV episodes? Hulu is where it's at. And if you're an HGTV addict, you'll definitely want to invest in Sling.

Like I mentioned before, each of these streaming options does require a Smart TV or a separate streaming device such as a Roku, Chromecast, Amazon Fire TV stick, Xbox, or Apple TV device to fully function, but it's just a one-time fee that is quickly recovered by going a few months without cable. Each device also comes with its own set of channels and shows included, and many don't even require a subscription to access.

READER TIP:

> *We have had Hulu and Netflix for two years and don't miss cable at all!*
>
> *—Katie, MD*

With streaming sites, subscription services, and special bundles popping up all over the place, it's easier than ever to say goodbye to cable, or at least find a better deal on your current package. Remember, prices and promotions may vary depending on the area you live in, and streaming sites, satellite services, and antennas are not always reliable in rural parts of the country, but it's worth experimenting to find the best entertainment option for your family.

We currently use an antenna for basic channels, Sling TV, and a Hulu subscription. With all three, we've never had to miss a favorite show, and I love that I can watch HGTV or Food Network episodes any time I want. This saves us approximately $387 per year over a regular cable subscription, and I couldn't be happier with the variety of entertainment we have at our fingertips!

DAY 13 ACTION PLAN

- If you currently have a cable subscription, call your provider and negotiate a better rate.
- Cut back to the most basic package, and watch shows via a TV network app or by borrowing entire seasons from the library.
- Eliminate your cable bill completely, and supplement with a streaming service combined with an antenna.

Day 14:
SAVE ON INTERNET SERVICES

While one might consider cable an unnecessary cost, the internet is a completely different story. It makes the world go 'round. We can surf websites, read the news, pay our bills, connect with friends and family on social media, and even order pizza. The internet has come a long way since the first introduction of the World Wide Web, and I, for one, am super thankful for its existence. Without it, I'd be out of a job rather quickly!

The addition of internet access on our phones only increases our dependence. Don't even get me started on the hundreds of available apps either. It seems anything and everything needs the internet to help it run, making this amenity extremely hard—no, impossible—to imagine living without.

We personally pay for our internet as a separate bill since we don't have a cable package to bundle it with, but still, we try to be pretty judicious with the cost. This might mean things like sacrificing speed or quality, but at the end of the day, we're almost always able to access exactly what we need to.

Plus, with the presence of free Wi-Fi in a variety of public places, I can always pop into the local library, coffee shop, or hotel parking lot if I need a change of scenery. That, or when the power goes out from one our infamous Florida thunderstorms!

Whether you pay for internet in a bundled package or as a separate bill like ours, here are five ideas to help you slash costs while still enjoying all the luxuries this amazing technology has to offer:

1. KNOW YOUR TERMS

I'm not super technical, so when I think of the internet, I think of it as one service that comes from one piece of equipment—the computer. This isn't so. In fact, I had to ask Joseph a whole bunch of questions again to figure out how all this internet stuff worked. Even though a lesson in definitions might not seem relevant to saving money, trust me, it is. You need to be knowledgeable about these terms so you know exactly what you're paying for, and what plan is best for you and your family!

Internet Options:

- **Dial Up** is typically what we think of when we remember the beginning stages of the internet, since it was the only thing available for a long time. Dial Up still exists, but in our image and video heavy culture, it's not ideal and very, very slow.

- **DSL** also runs through your phone line but is faster than Dial Up. You can still use your landline phone (if you have one) and be on the internet at the same time. Some DSL connections are not good for streaming video so if that is important, you will want to check the bandwidth of your DSL provider and compare it with the required bandwidth of your streaming service.

- **Cable** runs through your cable line and is offered by cable networks like Time Warner, Comcast, and BrightHouse. It isn't available everywhere, but when it is, it's usually much faster and more reliable.

- **Satellite** is provided by companies like DIRECTV and Dish. It usually comes with high-speed internet, but is also strongly affected by the weather. So you can expect your service to be spotty during heavy rains and snowfalls. It also requires a small satellite dish next to or attached to your home.

- **Wireless** does not mean Wi-Fi; instead it refers to systems that run off cell towers and charge by gigabyte (GB). Examples are wireless cards that plug into your computer or little "wireless hotspot" devices that create a mobile connection to the internet wherever you are. These can get expensive if they are your sole internet source, especially if you watch a lot of online videos. But if you just check email or only do an occasional web search, they actually might be cheaper than a DSL, satellite, or cable plan.

Gear You Need:

- **Modems** help process the signal into your home. DSL, satellite, and cable modems are not interchangeable.

- **Routers** create in-home W-Fi and allow multiple devices to use the internet at the same time.

- **Wireless Hotspots** do not need a modem or a router; these are the devices used by carriers like Verizon and AT&T for their wireless internet service.

And probably the most important term of all:

- **Mbps, or Megabits per second.** The higher the Mbps, the faster your internet, but you'll also pay more for your plan. Anything below 10 Mbps will most likely not be good enough for streaming TV shows on Netflix or Hulu, but would be fine for regular surfing. We currently have 10 Mbps and although it's not incredibly fast, it works for us and helps keep costs low.

  FYI: If your plan says Gbps, you have blazing fast internet. Unless you are an online gamer (or there is one in your house), you have plenty of room to cut back, and you won't even notice the difference.

As you research various bundles and plans, refer to these terms so you're not blindsided by a price or package you don't quite understand. Knowledge is power!

2. BUNDLE UP

Usually, you can get a better deal by combining your internet with a cable or phone package offered by the same company. But you should still read the fine print and do a little math before you make a final commitment.

Sure, you might get an awesome price for the type of service the company is offering, but do you really need to pay extra for 500 channels and a landline you'll never use? You have to make that call to see if it might be worth the additional rate.

For example, through one company in our area, you can get high-speed internet (20 Mbps) at a promotional rate for just $34.95. TV costs another $34.99, making that a total of $69.94 for both. But if you buy a bundle package, you can score both services for just $59.94 per month, or a savings of $10, which adds up to $120 per year. Granted, the internet bumps down to 10 Mbps with the package, but that's not a deal breaker when you can save that much!

Also, be aware of the 24-month commitment. Satellite companies in particular like to offer you a great rate for the first twelve months of a two-year commitment. If you sign one of these, know that your bill will probably skyrocket for months 13-24.

3. NEGOTIATE WITH YOUR PROVIDER

Similar to cable, a phone call to your internet company is a great way to haggle a lower cost. See if you can jump on any new customer promotions for a set time period and use a competitor's price as leverage to force their hand.

We did this when we faced a painful price hike after two years of loyal service to one company. Our bill jumped from $45 to $70/month—a considerable increase.

We called and explained that we really wanted to stay with them, but company X had a very enticing promotional rate of $39.95, and we were thinking of switching. Our original company bumped us down to $31 per month, which was $14 less than we were paying before. Now I only wish we had called them sooner!

READER TIP:

Our former internet company (who was sadly not available when we moved to another area) used *to offer a discount for loyal customers. They never advertised it, but whenever we were coming to the end of our promotion—usually twelve months—we would call them and ask to speak to someone in the customer loyalty department. We were always eligible for discounts and almost always paid $20 or less per month after they applied the discounts.*

—Lindsey, WA

4. BUY YOUR OWN MODEM

Internet providers often let you "rent" their modem for a set monthly fee, but this may or may not be the best deal depending on how long you will be using their service. A modem generally costs between $60-$100, so your internet company will make a killing after a specific time has passed.

Think about making this investment now, so you can save later, but be sure to consult with your provider before making any purchase. Most companies list exactly what kind of modem you need right on their website.

If you decide to switch companies based on a promotional rate, factor the cost of the modem in with your calculations as well. Like I mentioned before, DSL and cable modems are not interchangeable, and a different service may require a different modem.

5. EXPLORE ALTERNATIVE OPTIONS

Believe it or not, it *is* possible to get away without internet, and if the budget is tight, consider turning it off and jumping on a Wi-Fi connection whenever you need access. Local eating establishments, libraries, and even community parks have hotspots that are open to public use.

Some cell phone providers also let you use your phone as an internet hotspot. These plans are great for those who don't watch movies or download an insane amount of data. Always be sure to check with your phone provider, though, so you don't rack up extra fees and charges, and be sure to turn off your "spot" when you're finished to conserve battery and data.

However, using a public network does come with its own set of risks. Internet hackers can easily swipe your passwords and account information, so if you do activities like shopping and banking, save those tasks for when you're on a more secure network.

READER TIP:

I do not have internet, but I have unlimited data on my phone. I have a computer and tether my phone to my computer when we need it. Which is pretty rare—we do most things on my phone (or husband's phone, also unlimited) or at the library when we need to print (which isn't often yet).

—*Fayelle, GA*

I keep hoping worldwide Wi-Fi will become an option in the near future, but until then, we have to do whatever we can to cut this monthly expense. In the meantime, you can also help your internet pay for itself by using search engine reward sites like Swagbucks or Bing to pay you for things you usually do online anyway. I earn at least a $5 Amazon gift card every month when I consistently use these tools!

DAY 14 ACTION PLAN:

- Research your current plan, and make sure you understand internet jargon. Find out what plans and packages are offered based on what you need, and compare prices.

- Call your internet provider and negotiate a lower rate. Use a competing company's promotion package as leverage, if needed.

- Sign up for Swagbucks or Bing Rewards to earn gift cards while surfing the internet.

Day 15:
REDUCE YOUR PHONE BILL

Between landlines and smartphones, the average user is connected 24/7, with a cell sitting no more than a few feet away. Long distance isn't so much of a problem anymore, and minutes are mostly a thing of the past. And yet, we pay more than ever to have access to this technology!

Every day, I realize just how much more I can't live without this mini computer in my purse or back pocket. It's not only my instant connection to the outside world; it's also necessary for me to stay on top of my job. Plus, it's so convenient—the availability of data to access the internet, the convenience of texting over calling, and practically unlimited everything has spoiled me into never ever giving it up.

Still, I hate paying those astronomical prices, and I know most other phone owners do too. A personal or family phone plan usually makes up a significant portion of the budget, not to mention those nasty fees when a teen or two go over their monthly limit.

Thankfully, the phone market has shifted drastically over the past few years, with major players dropping two-year contract requirements, and smaller companies rising up with more affordable price points. Honestly, there's no better time than now to negotiate and lower your monthly phone bill, without getting rid of all the conveniences you've come to rely on and love.

Sure, you might have to sacrifice here and there—I'm still working on how much data I can live without—but more competition and more options mean there are also more ways to lower that bill. Here are my six favorite ways to cut back:

1. DITCH THE LANDLINE

If you still have a landline, first consider how often you really use it. Besides the excess sales calls, does it really warrant the addition of an entirely new phone contract and bill? Well, it depends.

One of the biggest arguments I hear for keeping a landline is for emergencies. When you dial 911 from a landline, the dispatcher can see your address right away. But when you call from a mobile device, the signal pings off of the closest cell tower, and takes much longer for the dispatcher to pinpoint an exact location. Even just a few seconds can feel like an eternity when you're facing an emergency.

If you have an elderly or disabled family member where 911 could be a real possibility, then by all means keep it, even if it's just for peace of mind. A very basic plan bundled with your cable and internet package is usually enough to get by. However, remember that when the power goes out, your phone will too, in which case you would have to use your cell. Weigh all the pros and cons, and decide whether or not a landline is completely necessary. For most phone users, it's not.

READER TIP:

> *I have a landline and no cell phone. It's $20.39 a month including taxes. I don't have long distance,*

caller ID, or call waiting, but I DO have unlimited minutes. It's still much cheaper than having a cell phone.

–Brandy, ThePrudentHomemaker.com

2. NEGOTIATE A BETTER RATE

If you've read the last few chapters, you should know by now that negotiation is your best tool for a lower bill. You never know what deal you can get unless you ask, so don't be afraid to call and see what your phone company has to offer.

- Talk through different scenarios and compare the final cost. For example, what happens when you have less data or limited texting?

- Inquire about various company or employee discounts that may be available. Some companies offer up to 27% off your total bill, which adds up over time.

- Explain that the cost is really high, and you would like to save a few extra dollars every month. Some companies will throw in a free perk like extra data for a few months to keep you as a customer.

My grandparents are expert negotiators, and I'll never forget the time I was with them in the Verizon store when they insisted on keeping the plan they already had, even though it didn't officially exist anymore. Verizon wanted them to "upgrade" to the new basic plan, which included more texts and minutes than they really needed, and cost a bit more too.

After much haggling, they walked out with the same plan they had been on at the same price, and I learned this lesson that day: Nothing is ever set in stone; everything is negotiable, so don't be afraid to try it for yourself!

However, *always* get your deal or negotiation in writing before you get off the phone or leave the store. Make note of the employee's name that you talked with, as well as the date and time you talked. We ended up paying more for a data plan than promised, and couldn't prove our case because we didn't keep detailed notes of our conversation.

3. USE A "DUMB" PHONE

It seems like everyone has a smartphone these days, but are they truly necessary? Sure, the apps are great, and internet access is even better, but if push comes to shove, you can survive on a phone that does a minimum of talk and text.

I actually remember the day I upgraded to my very own Android smartphone. I was way behind my peers, which bothered me a little bit, but the savings I experienced during those years of waiting were worth much more than the pressure. Joseph and I wanted to make sure we could actually afford the phone and extra data plan *before* we made the switch, because it was quite a jump when we did!

Since my job very much relies on internet access, I can't imagine going back now, but I also know that I would if I absolutely had to. So, if money is really tight, seriously consider using a phone with fewer capabilities...at least for a few months. You won't be tempted to check your email or Facebook feed every five minutes, and you'll save a bundle too.

4. CUT BACK WHERE YOU CAN

If having a smartphone is a non-negotiable, there are still a surprising number of ways to save on your cell phone plan if you're diligent about how much you actually use it. While unlimited talk, texting, and data sounds like a dream, it's also quite expensive. Look over your bill to see how much you're being charged for each of those items, and downgrade your plan for a lower rate.

This means you need to be conscious about staying under a certain minute or data package, which sounds hard at first, but you can actually save a lot of bandwidth just by surfing the internet and downloading apps on your own Wi-Fi network.

Also be aware of what apps are hogging the most data. This will mostly be in the videos you watch, pictures you upload, and any live streaming apps you use during the day, but you can also check the My Data Manager app to be absolutely sure. For texting, you can also use a free texting app, such as Text Me, to help stay under the allotted amount.

Regarding insurance, it's hard to say whether an extra monthly payment on your phone is actually worth it, especially since it's often accompanied with a $200 deductible. Since I have experience with a husband who has a habit of ruining phones, I tend to err on the side of caution, but you don't always have to pay for insurance through your specific carrier. SquareTrade.com offers a phone protection plan for less than $5/month, and only requires a $75 deductible if something breaks on your phone, or it dies completely.

READER TIP:

I recently became a SAHM, so we reduced our data plan from "unlimited" to 1GB per month. This alone is saving us $40/month! We don't need the same amount of data anymore since I'm home all day and can tap into our home Wi-Fi.

–Jennifer, MI

5. GO IN ON A FAMILY PLAN

Sometimes being independent is overrated, particularly if you're talking about a cell phone plan. Just think about the number of commercials you've seen over the past week that offer exceptional deals for added cell phone lines! It's worth combining forces to reduce your overall monthly cost.

Joseph and I used to pay a whopping $152 each month for both our smartphones, but saved $35 just by hopping on the same plan as my parents and grandparents. We had absolutely no changes to our data usage or minutes either!

See if a few family members or relatives would be willing to do the same—even a group of close friends is a great option and results in savings for everyone. Just be sure to work out all the payment details ahead of time, and even sign a contract, if needed. You don't want to risk ruining a relationship when money is involved.

6. SWITCH SERVICES

Let's say you've done everything you can to stay with your current company, but it's still not enough. You might want to seriously consider switching services and research AT&T, Sprint, T-Mobile, or Verizon to see what they can offer you.

There are also lesser-known (no-contract) plans that are becoming more popular every day:

- **Straight Talk** offers unlimited talk, text, and data, and runs off the Sprint, AT&T, and Verizon networks, depending on the area. You can save more money the longer plan you purchase (e.g., 30-day plan vs. a 365-day plan).

- **Ting** is a pay-as-you-go plan that works in "buckets." There are buckets of minutes, texting, and data, and you pay depending on how much you use. There is also a monthly device fee and it runs through the Sprint network.

- **Republic Wireless** also runs through the Sprint network, and works similarly to Ting. The difference, however, is that Republic Wireless will refund you the difference of whatever data you paid for but didn't use. They also don't charge you for individual minutes; you get unlimited talk and text for a flat fee.

You might be wondering whether the coverage for each of these plans will be adequate for your area. Talk to friends and family members who have experience with them, and compare notes to see if they might work for you too. Many of these pay-as-you-go plans offer coverage maps and usage calculators on their website so you can be absolutely sure before you commit.

It can be very confusing to navigate all the available options when deciding which phone plan is best for you. Focus on what you currently use, how much you have to use, and then do comparable research on available plans in your area.

Phone plans are always changing, but the awesome thing is, most carriers are getting rid of two-year contracts and focusing on more competitive options. That means you have a better opportunity to experiment with multiple plans without having to make a long-term commitment!

DAY 15 ACTION PLAN

- Look closely over your phone bill to see what you currently pay for each rate.
- If you're not on a family plan already, talk with your close friends and family members to see if a collaboration might be possible.
- Research some of the lesser known plans like Ting or Republic Wireless, and see how much your monthly payment would be using their on-line calculators.

Part 5: Reduce Medical Expenses

Day 16:
REDUCE HEALTH INSURANCE COSTS

While I try to live a healthy lifestyle, I don't feel comfortable doing it without health insurance. We have medications to pay for, doctor visits a couple times a year, and the occasional hospital emergency for the "uh-oh's" we never expected. We've definitely experienced our fair share of medical hot messes to know that going without just isn't an option!

Of course, that doesn't mean I'm willing to accept the cost of our monthly premium as a permanent fixture in our budget. Every time open enrollment comes around, it reminds me to do my due diligence and call around for quotes, making sure that I have the best plan possible for the best possible price. But lately, it seems like great coverage is getting harder and harder to find.

In fact, I think most of us would agree that the health care system is pretty broken. Unless you have an awesome job with a large company, monthly premiums are one hefty expense without a lot of benefits to go with it. And for people like Joseph and me who are self-employed, it's even harder to get that protection of health insurance without the huge cost.

Thankfully, the industry is starting to shift, and although it's not perfect, I think we're definitely headed in the right direction. Pre-existing conditions are pretty much non-existent anymore, and everyone can experience at least one preventive care visit a year at no cost. Low-income individuals now have access to more affordable plans, and patients, in general, have a little more control over what and how much they pay. I can only hope the future provides us with better and even more options down the road!

But until that magical health care system finally arrives (one that everybody agrees with, that is), there are a few changes you can make to your insurance plan so it doesn't hurt as much every month. It takes a little bit of research on the front end, and lots of experimenting, but it can be done. Here are five recommended ways to get the care you need for less:

1. REASSESS YOUR CURRENT PLAN

My instinct is to head straight for the cheapest insurance plan possible, but that's not always the best option. If you have a health problem that requires multiple doctor visits, prescriptions, and specialists throughout the year, you could actually pay hundreds more out of pocket in the long run, making it *cheaper* to hop on a higher premium plan.

To figure out that monthly premium sweet spot, look over your credit or debit card paper trail from last year, and add up all your medical expenses. Divide that by twelve to estimate your monthly health care cost, and use that number to determine the best plan for you. A higher out-of-pocket cost means you may want to increase your monthly premium and vice versa.

2. INCREASE YOUR DEDUCTIBLE

As with homeowner's and car insurance policies, the higher the deductible, the lower the premium. Sounds pretty straightforward, right? But remember, you are also taking a pretty big risk. If a major emergency happened, you'd automatically pay everything out of pocket until you met your deductible. Even then, your insurance might not cover everything in full after that.

Don't let this scare you! Sometimes a high deductible plan is the right choice. Here's how to know for sure:

- A high deductible plan is great if you very *rarely* get sick, and only make one doctor visit a year.

- It's also great if you have a hefty Emergency Fund in place to cover your deductible should you ever need to use it. Consider it insurance for your insurance!

For those enrolled in a high deductible plan, you can also open a Health Savings Account (HSA) to help pay for medical expenses. Contributions are tax free, tax deductible, and carry over from year to year.

READER TIP:

If you don't have an HSA through work, you can get your own HSA and 100% of what you put in there, depending on family or self-coverage limits, will be tax deductible. So for us, we have an HSA through Chase Credit Union and the max contribution for the year is $6,500. We then pay our medical expenses out of that account.

–Katie, UT

3. SEPARATE AND SAVE

While Joseph and I are on the same insurance plan now, it hasn't always been that way. He had insurance through a previous job, and although it wasn't the best plan ever, the price made it a no-brainer to participate. However, the cost would have more than tripled to add me to the policy!

We decided that the best course of action would be to put me on an entirely separate plan, and although I paid a pretty penny every month, it was much less than if we had doubled up on the same plan. This doesn't *always* happen, but it's enough to at least make a little research on the front end worth doing.

Experiment with a split policy among family members, then compare the final totals to see if you can score a cheaper rate. If you have children, see what it would cost for them to be a dependent under one spouse, separated under both, or on a government plan of their own. The results may surprise you!

4. PARTICIPATE IN WELLNESS INCENTIVES

Many health plans offer incentives for staying healthy, and will actually reward you for getting yearly checkups, or logging your exercise every day. When I worked as a bank teller, my health insurance gave us the chance to participate in quarterly challenges, and we could win gift cards or cash just for completing each task.

These incentives are usually available through employee-based programs, but some allow you to participate directly with your insurance company. Just log into or call your current insurance plan and ask about any wellness incentives they offer.

You can often receive discounts on fitness memberships or health products, depending on the type of insurance plan you have. Here are just a few examples:

- Percentage off or free gym membership
- Free trial of a weight loss program
- Percentage off yoga gear
- Percentage off acupuncture and chiropractic appointments
- Stop smoking discounts

Some of these programs are not available in every state and even though they're offered through your health insurance plan, they are often *in addition to* the coverage you currently have.

5. FIND A DIFFERENT PLAN

It does take time, but researching different health insurance policies and gathering quotes is a must if you want to save big. Just think—if you can save at least $10 a month on your premium, that's over $100 per year, which is incredibly worth it! While big box insurance companies are the most logical place to look, there are also lesser-known options that might work for you and your family, depending on eligibility.

For instance, the Affordable Care Act allows low-income individuals the opportunity to jump on a plan that was previously only affordable as a benefit for employees of a large company, which means you can get fairly decent coverage for less. If you're not familiar with Marketplace Insurance, you basically choose your plan based on income eligibility, and it's provided through a private insurance company. You pay the company your portion of the plan, and the government pays the rest as a tax credit.

Another option is Christian sharing ministries. With these types of plans, you pay the premium towards a member that needs medical help. While preventive care visits and prescriptions are paid out of pocket, any time your medical bills reach a certain threshold, you submit those needs to the ministry, and they are automatically paid by the membership.

Because it's easy to lose track of payments, visits, and procedures, I have found that it's best to keep good records of how much I was charged, how much my insurance covered, and how much I owe, to make sure nothing slips through the cracks. This is really helpful when you have a large deductible, so you know exactly how much it takes to meet it and you're never overcharged.

If you'd like a copy of the Medical Procedure Tracking Sheet I use, you can download it at

CreativeSavingsBlog.com/ExpenseResources

It's great for that at a glance look at how much you paid in medical bills throughout the year, and is helpful come tax time just in case you qualify for a medical deduction!

DAY 16 ACTION PLAN:

- Reassess your current plan, and figure out your insurance premium sweet spot. Remember to divide your yearly out-of-pocket medical expenses by twelve.

- See if any wellness incentives or discount programs are available through your current insurance company, and take advantage of them.

- Research alternative insurance plans to see if you can find one with a lower premium. Be realistic about the coverage you need so you don't pay too much!

Day 17:
SAVE MONEY AT THE DOCTOR'S OFFICE

I try to avoid the doctor's office like the plague. It could be a yearly checkup or nagging condition—either way, I hate going!

I know I really shouldn't say that, but the more I have to go to the doctor's office, the more copays I have to dish out… and ours are not the cheapest copays you've ever seen. Besides, every time I go I seem to lose a little more faith in the medical system. I'm not a conspiracy theorist or anything, and I *know* not every doctor is like this, but I'm frustrated by the number of treatments that focus only on the symptoms, rather than take the necessary steps to eliminate the actual problem.

This is why over all the money saving tips I'm going to share with you, preventive care is the most essential. Although this phrase is overused and sounds totally cliché, the "apple a day" thing does have some merit, and will keep you out of the doctor's office more than you think. Real food (fruits, veggies, and all that non-processed stuff), alleviate so many symptoms that prescriptions only cover up. In fact, I'm continually amazed at how good I feel when I've nourished my body the right way!

While a healthy lifestyle keeps you on the up-and-up, it still doesn't completely eliminate the need to see a doctor. With relentless allergies, an incapacitating bout of flu, or more severe medical cases like broken bones to contend with, some things are best left to the care of a professional... as they should be.

However, that doesn't mean you're left to pay whatever the doctor or insurance company deems acceptable. The next time you head to your local clinic, try one of these six ways to keep costs as low as possible, and save your hard-earned dollars for the real medical emergencies:

1. KNOW WHAT YOUR INSURANCE COVERS

Although most medical facilities will ask you what insurance you have before they make an appointment, it's your job to be absolutely sure the physician is within your network and what procedures you are allowed to have. Otherwise, you could be slapped with a big denial from your insurance company, and left owing a hefty bill.

I know the insurance manuals you get in the mail don't always read like an exciting novel, but one call to your insurance company and they are usually happy to walk through it with you. I like to take notes, clarify terms, and find out exactly what the deductible does and does not cover during the conversation.

I have referenced these notes many a time when doctors and hospital bills arrive in the mail, just to make sure all the amounts are correct. Depending on what's been covered, or if I have a question, I place another call to the insurance company. Sometimes the mistake has been on their end, and when they fix it, I get rebilled, or a nice little check in the mail!

2. NEGOTIATE AND PAY CASH

If you don't have health insurance, cash is the next viable option to pay for your visit. All doctors generally have a price sheet depending on the type of visit you have, so call around and get a variety of quotes before deciding which office to stop by. Just make sure that the doctor services uninsured patients. Some do, and some don't. Unlike hospitals, they're not required to by law.

When you confirm the average price for the doctor you're considering, call a couple insurance companies, or visit HealthCareBlueBook.com, and find out what they normally pay that doctor for that particular diagnosis. In case you were unaware, doctors charge far more per visit than they actually get paid—just one of the many secrets I learned while working for one!

With both amounts in hand, you're finally ready to negotiate a price for your visit. Be honest and see what price they can offer you before divulging your numbers. Most doctor's offices already have a discount they can offer you, and you may be able to whittle it down even further based on your due diligence.

DID YOU KNOW?

No matter which plan you purchase, preventive services are now free to all health care subscribers as a result of Obamacare. This includes yearly checkups and screenings.

3. TAKE ADVANTAGE OF FREE OR LOW-COST SERVICES

If you don't have health insurance, or come up short on cash, there are free or low-cost health clinics around the country that offer services to patients regardless of their ability to pay.

- NAFCclinics.org allows you to search for clinics near your zip code.

- For free breast exams and cervical screenings, you can find a local program through the CDC or Komen.org/Affiliates. These programs usually allow at least one checkup per year.

- Stop by Walgreens or CVS for common conditions such as strep throat, pink eye, and ear infections, just to name a few. These clinics offer lower costs outside a regular doctor's visit, and list a price sheet right on their websites so you know exactly what you have to pay.

Even a general Google search for "free or low-cost health care clinic" along with your state will pull up a variety of options so you can get the care you need, at a price you can afford.

4. PHONE IT IN

Whether you have an excessive allergy problem, weird rash, or pain, call your doctor before making the trek to see if they can help you over the phone. Of course, don't do this if it's a serious medical emergency! But if you're debating whether or not it's worth making an appointment, give your office a quick call first.

We actually did this during a bout of bad allergies, and because we have such a good relationship with our doctor, he graciously called in a medication for me without the need to go in for an appointment. I was incredibly relieved we didn't have to shell out a $60 copay!

You can also do this for follow-up appointments. Obviously, this decision is completely up to you and what you feel comfortable with. I'm not telling you not to go, but for me, when it's something minor or the issue is completely gone, I will call and see if I can stay home to avoid another copay. Be sure to check with the doctor first before making a final decision.

READER TIP:

Usually, we don't have to visit if I call and speak with the nurse. Nine times out of ten she tells me my kids will either be fine or what I should give them to help them feel better. We've even had the doctor call in meds without a visit by talking to the nurse. Even after hours many offices have a doctor on call.

–Brittany, MoneySavvyMomma.com

5. INSPECT YOUR BILL

When I worked in the billing department at an OBGYN office, I learned a whole lot about medical billing and coding. I also learned that what the patient pays, or whether or not the claim is even accepted by the insurance company, rests heavily on the coder. That's a lot of pressure!

It's obviously the billing department's responsibility to code your visit properly before submitting any claims, but it's up to you to make sure there's not a mistake. Some doctors will try to "upcode" the visit, meaning they assign it a more serious diagnosis so they get paid more. Sometimes they even submit claims for procedures that weren't even done.

If you end up being responsible for the bill, or it seems you owe more than you thought, call the office to request a second look, and make sure to ask if it could be a possible coding issue. They can fix it and resubmit your claim to see if that makes a difference. You can also search Google on your end to see what the code actually means—this will be a string of numbers on the bill from the doctor or hospital next to the date of service.

6. PRACTICE HOME CARE

Although not all medical problems require the services of a doctor, you have to weigh the pros and cons and decide for yourself whether or not to make the trip. And though you have to be careful about certain things you read on the internet, there *are* good sites and resources to help you try a medical remedy at home.

One of the more popular home remedies is essential oils. Even though they've only been recently trendy, they've been used medicinally for thousands of years. They work for so many things too!

There's a lot of debate about which oils to use and how to use them, but the best thing I can tell you is to be proactive about researching for yourself. Know what to look for in a quality oil, and purchase a reference guide to help use them properly. One of my favorites is the *Essential Oils Desk Reference* by Life Science Publishing.

Although I haven't specifically talked about dental or eye care services in this chapter, many of these principles can still be applied. The only other thing I would mention is not to discount a local dentistry or optometry school. Sometimes services are offered at 50% of the normal rates. Contacts and glasses can also be bought cheaper through a store like Walmart or Costco, rather than a private office.

I hope you don't think I'm completely anti-doctor, because I am definitely not! You don't have to avoid the doctor's office if you truly need it, but at least now you know how to make your dollars work a little harder when you do.

DAY 17 ACTION PLAN:

- If you're not positive about what your insurance policy covers, take some time to go over it and understand all the percentages, copays, and deductibles in full.

- Inspect your last medical bill to make sure it was coded and paid properly. Call your doctor with any questions if you're not sure.

- Make a healthy lifestyle choice. Go for a brisk walk or swap out a pre-packaged snack for a piece of fruit. It's better than doing nothing at all!

Day 18:
AVOID BIG HOSPITAL BILLS

I can't say I have a ton of experience with hospitals, which I guess is not only a good thing, it also means I can count on one hand how many times either Joseph or I have been in one. Between the two of us, we've experienced one appendectomy, one outpatient surgery, and a couple of broken bones, but other than that, nothing too major. I know—we're very lucky!

You would think our medical bills would reflect this, but instead, hospitals like to charge us more per visit than a week at a ritzy condo. If you had seen any of our local facilities at the time, you would know that description does not fit...*at all.*

Unfortunately, hospitals charge for anything and everything these days, from a two-minute visit to a small dose of Advil. Even the doctor who sees you can charge you in addition to what the hospital does. I understand that everyone should get paid for their time, but this type of price gouging is absolutely ridiculous. It's no wonder we quickly find ourselves buried under a huge medical and financial mess.

In fact, just this past summer, we experienced our first cancer scare (which turned out to be nothing, thankfully!), but it did mean we had a lot more mail from specialists and surgeons than we were used to. The cost to get everything resolved completely depleted our Emergency Fund and then some, and a few months later, I was still paying off all the expenses we incurred.

While it's something I would never want to go through again, this experience showed me just how much a small problem can escalate into a major cost. That means it's even more important to cut where we can, and prevent big hospital bills in the future. These five tips will show you exactly how and where to start:

1. TRY A WALK-IN CLINIC

Depending on your insurance, a trip to the ER could cost you anywhere from $100 to $500. Sometimes, these fees are waived if you're actually admitted to the hospital, but don't count on that being a sure thing. A lot of problems can be solved right on the ER floor, which means you're still responsible for that hefty fee.

The next time you have a medical emergency that isn't too serious, try going to a walk-in clinic or urgent care first. Most clinics have the capability to do x-rays and prescribe the medication you need, and will refer you to the hospital if they think it's truly necessary.

We did this before Joseph's appendectomy, or at least before we knew that's what the problem was. We weren't sure why he was having so much pain, but rather than risk a costly ER visit after our primary's hours, we went to urgent care. They were able to diagnose the problem, and promptly sent us to the hospital without the need to wonder what was going on or wait for results. We also only owed the clinic a small copay, and avoided the ER fee since Joseph was admitted for surgery.

2. CALL AROUND FOR PRICES

Every hospital has a different billing price for each procedure, and these can vary greatly whether the hospital is located in the same city, or a few hours away. If you're considering any sort of surgery or hospital service, place a few calls to see where you can get the best deal. Obviously, the credibility and reputation of the doctor is number one, but it doesn't hurt to shop around just in case you need to negotiate later.

Remember, there are always additional costs like anesthesiologists, x-ray techs, and various medications in addition to the surgeon, so don't forget to gather prices for each of those itemized charges as well. HealthCareBlueBook.com will quickly do this for you.

Make sure absolutely everything is considered in-network for your insurance. If you go out of network, you could encounter thousands more than you were originally expecting. Some insurance plans pay less for out-of-network hospitals and doctors, or they may not pay anything at all. Call your insurance company, and make sure the specific hospital and/or doctor you use are approved before the next medical emergency.

DID YOU KNOW?

Hospitals are required to serve and treat all patients whether they have insurance or not.

3. NEGOTIATE AND PAY CASH

Like we talked about in the chapter regarding doctor visits, if you don't have health insurance, try paying cash. Many doctors are more willing to work with you if you have the ability to pay with cold hard cash. You can also contact the financial services department and see if they have a "prompt pay" discount, which means you get a discount just for paying the bill in its entirety that day.

Even if you have insurance, a high-deductible plan is not going to cover much. Did you know you can still negotiate a lower rate? I recently read a story from a reader of GetRichSlowly.com, and she retold her experience of whittling a $2,300 ant bite down to $1,100. Of course, that's still a lot for an ant bite, but she scored a little more than a 50% discount just for being nice to the hospital rep on the phone.

If all else fails, there's no shame in asking to be put on a payment plan with your hospital. Most are willing to set up a plan for you interest free, which alleviates a lot of financial pressure when you can't afford to pay all in one day. Be careful, though, as you don't want to get caught up in the cycle of medical debt. Keep track of payments on your end with a payment schedule of your own. Then get rid of any debt as soon as possible!

4. DISPUTE YOUR BILL

We've all heard stories about hospitals charging for some of the most outrageous things, such as $800 for an aspirin or $1,000 for a doctor checking in on you for less than one minute. It's good to get these fees broken down into an itemized list on your bill, so you can see exactly what was done and how much it cost. If something doesn't look right to you, don't be afraid to call and have the hospital clarify.

On the other hand, if you're charged for something that you consider a mistake, call to see if you can get a discount or have the charge completely waived. We actually had an emergency room fiasco a few years ago where I was *not* admitted because they didn't think my eye issues were that serious, when actually they were, as determined by the ophthalmologist I saw the following day.

I was able to get my $100 emergency room fee waived because I wrote a letter signed by my eye doctor to the hospital, explaining the situation and that I shouldn't be held responsible for the fee. It took a few months of phone calls and haggling, but I eventually got the entire fee waived.

READER TIP:

You need to do your due diligence upfront. Find out what your insurance will and will not cover first (do you have an 80/20 plan or will your insurance cover 100% after the deductible is met) and find out what your doctor's policies are. Does your doctor require an upfront payment of your deductible or if you're having a baby, can you pay after you deliver? Make sure you know the answers to these questions as early as possible to avoid a huge and unexpected upfront payment.

—*Jessi, TheBudgetMama.com*

5. DON'T PAY THE ENTIRE BILL UPFRONT

Despite how good it normally is to pay your bills upfront and on time, it's not always that way when it comes to the hospital, especially if you have a deductible you have to meet first. With my biopsy, the hospital wanted me to pay for the entire procedure before it was done, but I knew my previous mammogram and lab work would go towards my deductible, thus lowering my actual responsibility.

I politely declined and explained my reasoning, and they didn't have a problem with it at all. Sure enough, when the charges eventually came through my insurance company, I actually owed less to the hospital than they initially told me.

Even though the hospital may try to boss you around, you have more negotiating power than you think. The next time they ask you to pay everything upfront, don't give in, and let it run through your insurance first!

Often when you take an emergency (or even planned) trip to the hospital, you leave with a ton of paperwork. There are bills from the doctor, the hospital, anesthesiologist (if you needed one), lab work, and any other tests that were done. It can get out of hand rather quickly!

Keep a file of all the medical bills and insurance claim paperwork you receive, and group them based on each medical-specific visit. This is extremely helpful in case you need to reference something later, and has actually saved us money. We avoided an anesthesiologist payment because the hospital billed it to our insurance too late, and we were able to prove this via the paperwork we had neatly filed away.

DAY 18 ACTION PLAN

- Take a few minutes to research walk-in clinics closest to your home, and pop the number and address into your phone's contact list so you'll always have it with you.

- Call your insurance company so you know which hospitals are considered in-network for your plan.

- If you have a medical bill you still owe money on, find out what an average procedure cost is for your area, then call the hospital to negotiate a lower rate.

Day 19:
LOWER PRESCRIPTION DRUG COSTS

There was a period in time when both Joseph and I didn't have any health insurance at all. He had started a new job, and we were surprised to find out the waiting period was at least three months before the insurance plan kicked in. There wasn't much else we could do besides put ourselves on the "don't get sick" plan, and try to avoid dangerous situations that could result in a broken bone—not that we seek these opportunities anyway! What we didn't know was how we were going to afford the medications I was on in the meantime.

It was during these three months that I did a *ton* of research on how to cut costs and make prescriptions affordable. But pharmacies didn't always want to work with us, and the costs for certain meds were still really, really high. Even now, the insurance plan I have requires a fairly high deductible before any of the copays kick in. This, paired with a long list of side effects, often makes me wonder whether it's worth taking any medication at all!

Maybe you've been in, or currently find yourself in a similar spot. I know it can feel like you're trapped in an endless cycle—you need your prescription, but you can't afford it. Then you either fall further behind in your bills, or take dangerous measures like skipping doses and cutting pills in half without talking to your doctor first.

No matter what your prescription situation looks like right now, there's always a way to trim this portion of your budget, even if it's just a little. You don't have to settle for full price anymore, not when there are so many affordable options available to you!

1. ASK FOR SAMPLES

If you don't have insurance, or have a high deductible, it never hurts to ask for free samples at the doctor's office. This is especially helpful if you are prescribed a new medication and don't know the cost of it yet, or don't have time to shop around.

Pharmaceutical reps are *always* pitching doctors new meds, and often leave samples behind for patients to try. It might not be as much as they used to (company spending on samples has gone down 25% since 2007)[10], but as long as they're just sitting in cabinets, you might as well take advantage of them! I would say I've had about an 80% success rate when asking my doctor for a free sample.

If doctors don't have the samples you need on hand, ask if they would be willing to order some. Many pharmaceutical companies or prescription-specific websites feature a section where health care professionals can put in a sample request.

2. TAKE ADVANTAGE OF DISCOUNT DRUG CARDS

Prescription savings cards are the next best option if you don't have insurance, and there are hundreds of them out there. It never hurts to print out a few and see which ones will give you the greatest discount. I saw savings anywhere between $20-$60 when we used ours!

Here are the ones I recommend you try first:

- BetterRxCard.com
- TogetherRxAccess.com
- NACoRx.org
- RxAssist.org
- RxSavingsPlus.com
- FloridaDiscountDrugCard.com - FL residents only
- BigAppleRx.com - NYC residents only
- APharmaCard.com
- TrueRxSavings.com

Beware, not every pharmacy takes these cards, so call around before you order a script so you don't end up paying full price.

READER TIP:

My family also uses a prescription discount card. None of us have regular prescriptions to fill, so we don't have that option added to our insurance plan. But it's still been nice to save money for when we do need one!

—Olivia, MD

3. USE A COUPON

If you prefer to use a brand-name drug, or don't have access to a generic brand, do a quick Google search for the manufacturer's website to print off coupons. I found one for my current prescription within minutes, and even though a $10-$15 coupon doesn't sound like much, every little bit helps!

Another site to check is InternetDrugCoupons.com. There are hundreds of medications listed, so it's worth a look. One thing to remember, though, is if you have insurance, you probably won't be able to use these coupons on top of your coverage. They are only eligible for those without.

Although this isn't a coupon per se, you may want to look into AstraZeneca to see if you're eligible for their prescription savings program. This company probably sounds familiar as it's tacked on to the end of almost every prescription based television commercial, but it provides medications at no cost to patients who need them.

4. GO GENERIC

I know this sounds like a no-brainer, but if you have the chance to go generic, you should seriously consider it. Generic drugs are considerably cheaper than brand-name, and there's a very good chance it won't affect you any differently than the more expensive brand.

In fact, many doctors assure their patients that it *is* the same, but I actually interviewed a pharmacy tech for a magazine article once, and she helped me understand that it's not always that simple. While the drug is essentially the same, they each carry fillers that react differently depending on your particular genetic makeup.

This is why after reading multiple reviews on how the generic version of my prescription affected everyone in different ways, I chose to stick with the brand-name until I didn't need it anymore. Would the generic have affected me any differently? I can't say for sure, but that decision is for people to decide for themselves. Do your research, consider the costs (and alternatives), and make the best decision for you!

5. USE A MAIL-ORDER PHARMACY

For insurance holders, a three-month supply of prescriptions ordered through a mail-order pharmacy is convenient and saves a ton of money. Because the pharmacy only dispenses the medication once, rather than three or more times, you're charged a lower copay. And most refills are simple to do online.

Here's the thing, though...you need to plan for mail-order drugs. If you order them too early, insurance won't pay for them and the online pharmacy won't give any out. But, if you wait too long, you might not receive the meds in time. Some take only a few days to send, while others can take up to two weeks. Mark your calendar so you know exactly when to order!

Check online sites like HealthWarehouse.com and FamilyMeds.com just to see if their prices are any lower. And for those who are intrigued by the "black market," I can tell you that I've had friends order their scripts from Canada with no problems, but you do have to be careful. It's harder to know which companies are legal, and which medications are truly authentic.

6. PAY FOR A SMALLER AMOUNT OF PILLS

If push comes to shove, and you really can't afford a thirty or ninety-day supply of meds, ask your pharmacist if they will separate the pills into smaller amounts to make payments more manageable.

$100 a month for medications can be steep if you're on a tight budget or have fallen into the donut hole, but $25 a week is a lot more manageable, especially if you're living paycheck to paycheck or are on a limited income.

You could also ask the doctor if they would be willing to prescribe a larger dose that you can then cut in half. The dispensing fee (a.k.a. your copay) will be the same, but you'll get more meds for your dollar.

JUST TO CLARIFY:

> **Donut Hole:** *For those enrolled in Medicare Part D, you may have heard the term "Donut Hole." This refers to the gap when Medicare patients were required to pay 100% of their prescription drug costs after reaching a certain spending level, and would last until they had spent $4,500 (2014) out-of-pocket. The Affordable Care Act is slowly shrinking this gap and allowing for more discounts and provisions for those inside the donut hole until it can get rid of it entirely.*

7. ENROLL IN A REWARDS PROGRAM

If for some reason your insurance doesn't offer a mail-order option, or you don't have a regular prescription to fill, consider a pharmacy that offers loyalty rewards.

- Walgreens adds 100 points to your Balance Rewards card every time you fill a prescription. 5,000 points = $5.

- CVS gives $5 in Extra Buck Rewards for every ten prescriptions.

- Target gives 5% off an in-store purchase after you fill five prescriptions.

However, big box stores like Walmart and Costco might ultimately offer better prices and copays than you would receive in rewards, so definitely make a few calls before settling on your go-to pharmacy.

If you have an employee-based health plan, it doesn't hurt to check and see if they offer a Flexible Spending Account or Health Savings Account. Although these are getting more and more rare (ours was eventually taken away in NY), FSA's and HSA's allow you to set aside tax-free dollars for use in prescription payments, copays, and sometimes even deductibles. You would be surprised by how much you can save in just taxes on these types of expenses, so it's worth asking!

DAY 19 ACTION PLAN

- Ask for samples of your medication from the doctor the next time you see him/her, or print out a discount drug card or coupon and use it the next time you fill a prescription.

- Switch to a mail-order pharmacy if your insurance company offers one, or look for an online pharmacy that's reputable and provides a good rate.

- Sign up for a pharmacy reward program if you haven't already, or check to see if your current pharmacy offers one.

Part 6:
Reduce Personal Care Expenses

Day 20:
SAVE MONEY ON MAKEUP

Part of me wishes I were born with an affinity for all things makeup and hair. I watch beauty vloggers turn back the clock with ease and think, "I can totally do that!" In reality, I stand in front of the mirror and use foundation that ends up being the wrong color, or smear my already thick eyeliner.

"It's gotta be the products," I say to myself, "I just don't have the right products." Which of course convinces me to buy the most expensive brands out there hoping it will change the outcome. I'll let you in on a little secret...it doesn't.

However, it *does* mean I've tried all sorts of foundations, mascara, blush, lipstick, and eyeliner (in multiple brands) to get the look I want. I still wouldn't call myself a makeup expert, but after years of practice and experimentation, I finally have a morning makeup routine that takes about five minutes from start to finish. It's definitely not over the top, and I probably don't even use most of the products properly, but it works for me in the stage of life I'm in right now. At this point, I just want to apply it and go!

While I'm certainly not opposed to using a pricier product, my search for the best has revealed you don't have to spend a fortune to get the quality you need. If you're looking for ways to cut down on beauty costs, and still create a natural, effortless look, these six ideas are a must try:

1. USE WHAT YOU HAVE (OR RETURN IT!)

Am I the only one who seems to forget I have unused makeup stuffed in a back drawer? Usually it's from an impulse buy or a drugstore sale I couldn't resist, but if I would only remember to check my own stash, I probably wouldn't need to buy any new makeup for months!

If by chance you have a secret drawer of unused makeup products yourself, go through it and ruthlessly purge what you don't like or won't ever wear. Then make it a habit to always check that bin before adding a new product to your grocery list. Many times, I've forgotten what I threw in there, and am completely surprised to find unopened products just waiting to be used.

However, if you *do* buy something, and end up not liking it at all, don't hesitate to take it back. I regularly purchase makeup from Target, Ulta, and Mary Kay, and they all have very generous return policies. You can exchange just about anything you've already opened!

2. BUY FROM THE DRUGSTORE

Drugstore prices do not always mean it's a bad product. I have found several inexpensive brands that are preferable to higher quality labels. Plus, you can always find coupons for makeup in the Sunday paper or online to combine with store sales, meaning you almost never have to pay full price.

To avoid purchasing a dud, do a little research online before heading to the store. You can Google "best drugstore concealer" or something similar, and find even more information on a specific product just by adding "review" to the end of the name. Thousands of beauty bloggers and vloggers make their living testing and showcasing makeup products, so one of them is bound to feature what you're looking for.

Another tip: don't be afraid to take a bottle of your current makeup with you when you go shopping. Comparing colors is the best way to make sure you buy the right product the first time around, especially when it comes to foundation, so try to match it as best you can before heading to the check-out line.

READER TIP:

If you have a Dollar General or Big Lots, check there. I have scored big on Olay BB Cream at Big Lots. They have big brand names there for less. Dollar General is hit or miss but great for beauty supplies for your face. Every now and then they have clearance on makeup and that is a WIN.

—*Allison, VA*

3. GO DOUBLE-DUTY

You don't have to stuff your makeup bag with separate bottles of moisturizer, primer, foundation, and sunscreen anymore. Instead, you can grab a cream that rules them all by doing double, sometimes triple duty!

Here are the most popular options:

- Tinted Moisturizer – A tiny bit of color mixed with a moisturizing cream

- BB Cream – Light foundation coverage with moisturizer and sunscreen

- CC Cream – A lighter foundation that helps even skin tone
- DD Cream – Claims to do everything the previous creams do, though it was created with extremely dry skin in mind

These creams are best used by those who don't need (or prefer) a ton of coverage, so you will want to experiment with a couple samples before immediately jumping in.

Also, foundation-like products are not the only ones with more than one job to do. There are eye creams with primer included, nourishing lipsticks that don't require lip balm underneath, and blush sticks that work for both the cheeks and lips. Once you start down the makeup aisle, you might be pleasantly surprised that you don't need as many products as you originally thought!

4. MAKE IT YOURSELF

Believe it or not, the store isn't the only place you can get cosmetics; you can also make them yourself! There are hundreds of DIY recipes that use everyday ingredients and are completely free of harmful toxins.

All you have to do is stock up on sterilized empty jars with tight fitting lids (you can find clear ones on Amazon.com), then browse Pinterest to find replacement recipes for your favorite finds.

In one five-minute search I printed off recipes for makeup remover, mineral makeup, eyeliner, concealer, and even natural lipstick. Best of all, they cost pennies compared to more expensive brands.

A word of caution, though—because homemade makeup products don't contain any preservatives, you'll need to keep some of them in the fridge so bacteria won't have a chance to grow. They also need to be replaced more often.

5. GRAB FREE SAMPLES

One of my favorite ways to try new makeup is through free samples. Even though most stores have those generous return policies we talked about before, I hate spending money in the first place for something I'm not even sure I'll use.

MoneySavingMom.com or Freebies4Mom.com are sites to keep an eye on, and sign up when beauty freebies are available. Sephora, Smashbox, and Ulta also allow you to add samples to your online cart before checking out. And don't forget to check with your Mary Kay consultant too.

Even though these are mostly for one-time application purposes, I can usually squeeze at least two to three uses out of them, which means I can go longer in between makeup purchases!

READER TIP:

I love using ELF products. You can find them at Target or online for only $1-$3, and some of them are REALLY great. I love their tweezers, eye shadow, lip glosses, tinted moisturizers, so many things! I also subscribe to Ipsy for $10 a month to satisfy my craving for samples and other goodies.

—Krystal, SunnySweetDays.com

6. BE COSMETIC CONSCIOUS

Possibly the most important way to stretch cosmetic purchases is to stop using sponges. Yep, you heard me right!

These tiny tools actually waste your makeup by soaking in most of the liquid before you can even get it on your face. Use a clean finger or foundation brush to help make a little go a long way.

It's also good to use up ALL your product before throwing bottles in the trash. Because I don't like wasting anything, I'll try to squeeze every last drop out of my foundation that I can, and run my brushes through broken eye shadow until there are almost no crumbs left. I kind of make a game out of it to see how much I can use before I have to throw it away and buy new. It's always shocking how many more applications I can get out of each product whenever I do this!

You can even go as far as to cut off the tops of squeeze bottles or remove plastic pumps to continue using the make-up after it stops coming out of the dispenser. A tiny beauty spatula is perfect for this, and I'm always surprised by just how much product is left inside.

Makeup is not a necessity, but it can do wonders to help you feel a little more YOU. In fact, I love how expert makeup artist and business owner, Bobbi Brown, explains it, "Make-up is a way for a woman to look and feel like herself, only prettier and more confident." And now that you know all the savings secrets, you don't have to spend a fortune to look your best!

DAY 20 ACTION PLAN:

- Spend five minutes going through your makeup stash and throw out everything you know you won't use, including expired products.

- Take inventory of what you *do* need, then pop on over to Google to find the best cosmetics for less. Keep an eye out for free samples!

- Find a DIY makeup recipe on Pinterest and gather all the ingredients you need to make it. Have fun experimenting!

Day 21:
AFFORD ALL THINGS HAIR CARE

Even though I'm a frugal girl through and through, I rarely "cheap out" when it comes to my hair. It's not that I *haven't* tried to go to a hairdresser who charges less; it's just that I've never had good experiences with chain salons. The cut is always uneven, the color a tiny bit off, and then I end up spending even more money trying to get it fixed at a professional salon. Not to mention all the pints of ice cream I eat to soothe my emotions during the process!

Dollar shampoos and conditioners provide even worse results. It doesn't matter if the bottle promises soft and luscious locks, I always end up looking like a frizzy monster after using them. Nope, I'll gladly pay a pretty penny for a professional stylist and products that actually work with my hair. I don't even care if you think I'm vain.

You see, for me, hair care is a very important part of my overall well-being. I'm a much happier and more confident person when my hair actually does what I tell it to, and I bet many of you feel the same way. We as women want to feel and look pretty, but that doesn't mean we're opposed to saving money either. Especially if we can achieve similar results.

I'm happy to say you can have financial peace without sacrificing quality. These fantastic tips will help you save even more at the salon, *and* make those everyday hair products you already love and use at home a no-brainer to buy:

1. REDUCE SALON FRILLS

I mentioned before how important it is to find a good stylist, especially if you are super picky with your hair. However, there are still ways to save on the services you do need, and that's by reducing the services you actually get.

Here are a few tips and tricks:

- If you absolutely have to cover those greys, go for color instead of highlights. It's usually a little bit cheaper.

- If you do get highlights, opt for half a head instead of a whole. This stretches your money further and creates a much more natural effect.

- Get a cut/style that you don't have to trim every four to six weeks so you can go longer in between visits.

- Arrive with your hair already washed, or leave before the blow-dry. This shortens the service time and cost.

- Don't be coerced into deep conditioning treatments or add-on products. Prices are marked up and you can easily do the same thing at home.

If you don't have a stylist you're thrilled with, ask for recommendations from friends whose hair you *do* like, and see if the salon has any discounts for new customers. The majority also have referral programs so you can earn a free or discounted haircut just for telling your friends.

2. LEARN TO CUT HAIR

It took about seven years, but I finally convinced Joseph to let me cut his hair. He is pretty particular about getting a good cut, and even though it would save us about $16 every few weeks, he still insisted on going to a barber. Well, no more. Now he claims that I can give him a better-looking cut than the stylist ever did!

If you want significant savings and also have a few boys in the house who don't mind your practicing on them, learn to cut their hair. You'll need a nice pair of hair scissors and a set of clippers for a more professional cut, but once you invest in those tools, you'll get years of use out of them. You can also give your own bangs a trim instead of stopping by the salon for a five-minute snip.

I recommend watching a few YouTube tutorials first, based on the type of cut you want to do. I found this extremely helpful in knowing exactly where to start!

READER TIP:

We cut everyone's hair at home. My husband cuts his own and I cut the bottom edge and around his ears for him. We take turns cutting the boys' hair. I cut the girls' hair. He cuts my hair. I went a year without having it cut, as we didn't have money for me to get it cut that year, and it had become so long that I decided to have him give cutting it a try. He does a great job and the savings for nine people on haircuts is significant!"

—*Brandy, ThePrudentHomemaker.com*

3. PREVENT DAMAGE

Maintaining a healthy head of hair slows down the need for a trim and keeps you from taking an extra trip to the beauty chair. If you think you can get away with it, don't wash or shampoo your hair every day—excess washes strip your hair of its natural oils and harsh shampoos containing ingredients like sulfate are rough on your hair. You can use a sprinkle of dry shampoo or baby powder on the "off" days if you're worried about grease and buildup.

Heat can also damage hair pretty badly and cause major split ends, so opt to let your hair dry naturally after the shower if at all possible. If you can't go without (I know my waves get a little out control if I don't!), use a heat protectant spray before blow drying and straightening hair to keep it nice, smooth, and the moisture completely locked in.

And lastly, don't ever rub your hair with a regular towel after stepping out of the shower. An old t-shirt or special microfiber towel is softer on the hair, incredibly absorbent, and creates a lot less frizz.

4. SCORE A GREAT DEAL

If you have a brand-name product you buy over and over again, there's almost always a coupon available for it. Buy the Sunday paper or browse Coupons.com—even a quick Google search limited to the last week will bring up hundreds of results. You can also stretch your dollars even further if you match your coupon with a store sale or special gift card offer.

Although I've never scored a completely free bottle of shampoo or conditioner, I *have* saved some serious money on higher end items. I even bought four bottles of my favorite hairspray once because I had a couple coupons with me and there was a $5 gift card promo involved too. It only takes a few minutes to clip and scan the current week's ads, and since they're products you would use anyway, it's worth the minimal effort.

If you consider yourself a little more daring and don't mind trying different brands, sign up for FREE beauty samples at MoneySavingMom.com and Freebies4Mom.com. They offer mini packets of shampoo, conditioner, color creams, and styling products that don't cost anything but your name and email address. Most samples take between four to six weeks to be sent, but you should be able to get two or three uses out of them when they finally arrive!

READER TIP:

Those high-end shampoos are so worth it, but like all shampoos they are super concentrated. To get way more mileage out of that bottle, take an empty clean shampoo bottle with a flip top and fill it 1/3 to 1/2 full with shampoo. Top it off with lukewarm water and gently shake. Use this to wash your hair. Not only will it last longer, it is also better for your hair and will distribute more evenly.

—Monique, Netherlands

5. BE RESOURCEFUL

Have you ever read the directions on the back of your shampoo bottle? Most of them encourage you to lather, rinse, and repeat, but one cycle is more than plenty. In fact, most shampoos are so highly concentrated that you can actually water them down, and still get all the benefits.

For those who like to experiment with homemade products, take five minutes to browse Pinterest and collect an assortment of make-your-own recipes. There's homemade shampoo, detangler, hair gel, hair masks, even styling cream, and all use natural ingredients that are free of harmful toxins and are most likely already inside your pantry. Your hair might need a bit of an adjustment period since it will likely react to the lack of chemicals, but this is completely normal. It should go back to "playing nice" after a week or two, and can be much healthier long-term.

Also, just like we talked about in the makeup chapter, don't be afraid to cut off tops and dispensers to get an extra shampoo or styling application out of the bottle after you "think" you're done with it. The amount of product left inside can usually get you through two or three more treatments!

Spending more on our appearance seems justifiable no matter how much you spend, but I hope I've been able to prove that you don't have to give up your favorite products or beauty indulgences just to save a buck. There are plenty of other opportunities to cut costs and still make a big difference!

DAY 21 ACTION PLAN

- If you can get away with it, skip your next hair appointment or call and schedule it for a later date.

- Look for and clip hair related coupons from Coupons.com or the Sunday paper.

- Watch a hair cutting tutorial on YouTube and give your hubby and/or boys their next haircut.

Day 22:
TRIM YOUR TOILETRIES

Toiletries—a.k.a. toothpaste, deodorant, shaving cream, razors, lotions, etc.—are far from being considered a major expense, especially when you have bigger things to worry about like insurance and utilities. But...that still doesn't mean they can't make a big difference!

In fact, toiletries are some of the easiest products to save on because brand-name items are almost always on sale. Find a coupon to use on top of that, and you can secure yourself an amazingly great deal and pay practically pennies per item. But even if you don't have the time, energy, or desire to coupon, you can still save up to 40% with generic brands that work almost exactly the same way.

The other nice thing is you don't have to replace toiletries all that often. Many products last at least three to four months before you have to buy them again, although to be completely honest, I probably use them for much longer than that. My very blunt razor comes to mind as the most recent example!

Basically, though, this particular category is filled with loads of savings opportunities you'd be crazy not to take, and the following ideas will help you fill that toiletry cabinet for a lot less. Consider it the best way to save money on what you need, so you can put the extra cash towards something you actually want!

1. STOCK UP WHEN YOU SEE A SALE

Like I previously mentioned, sales on toiletry items happen *all* the time. It doesn't matter whether you're at Target, Walmart, or the closest drugstore, at least one or two brands have discounted their products to entice you to buy.

The best part is when you can find a coupon to match with the sale and make the deal even sweeter. Although scouring every deal matchup site and buying a Sunday paper every week is certainly an option, you don't have to go through such extremes to save a few bucks. Just take a quick peek at Coupons.com to see what's available, and only print coupons on items you already buy.

Then it's time to stock up.

And no, I don't mean fill your closets and cabinets with fifty packages of toothpaste, but sales are cyclical so you can expect to see them again every six to eight weeks. Plan accordingly and buy enough to get you through to the next sale.

2. BUY ONLINE

I don't always think about Amazon as *the* place to purchase toiletries, but a closer look reveals that it's a top competitor not to be ignored. And of course, why wouldn't it be? Amazon sells practically everything!

For example:

The deodorant I use is usually between $3-$4 per stick at the regular store. But on Amazon, I can buy a pack of 4 for just $7.98, making them $1.99 each. That's almost a 50% savings!

There is also a Prime Pantry option for those who are Amazon Prime members. How it works is you fill a box with as many Prime Pantry items as you need (this includes other household and grocery items in addition to toiletries), and it ships for $5.99 per box no matter how many products you put inside. This service is geared towards those who prefer to buy single-package options at regular price, rather than buy each item in bulk.

Another perk of Amazon is the ability to use their version of coupons. All you have to do is click on "Today's Deals" right underneath the search bar, and it will bring up another navigation bar on the next page. Look for the "Coupons" category and click on that to bring up hundreds of dollars worth of savings. The best part is they only require one little click, and that coupon is automatically applied to your shopping cart!

3. BUY IN BULK

The next time you're at Costco, Sam's Club, or BJ's, take a peek into the health and beauty section to crunch some numbers. Because toiletries don't go bad, it's easier to buy a pack of razors in bulk than it is to buy something like yogurt. And even though you can't generally use a coupon at these types of stores, it still ends up being a lot cheaper if you can't find the item on sale anywhere else.

Warehouse stores come with a yearly membership fee, but you can easily make your money back and more by going in with a family member or friend to share the discount. Just go shopping together every couple of months to get what you need, and split the savings. You can even split bulk items packaged together if you don't see yourself using that much in a year. Giant bottles of mouthwash and body wash sometimes take a long time to finish up, depending on how many you have in your family using them!

Another option is to consider a service like Dollar Shave Club or 99¢ Razor. While both offer subscription options (meaning you get razors delivered to you every month or every other month), 99¢ Razor also offers a bulk option for those who don't want to be signed up for a monthly fee. The prices are really affordable, and the quality is outstanding. Joseph has used the same blade for up to four months and still had a sharp cut!

READER TIP:

We use mouthwash, flossers, and toothpaste (name brands too!) from the dollar store. We like the Sam's Club brand of toilet paper, and I buy Dove bar soap and body wash there too (my son has eczema & that brand works best for him). We are Plus members and they have a sale on them every few months.

—Lisa, VA

4. SWITCH TO A CHEAPER ALTERNATIVE

Cheaper brands often get a bad rap when compared to items like dentist recommended Crest and Colgate, but it's worth trying a few different labels just to see what you like best. Sometimes, the less expensive and generic option can be a surprising win!

In the same fashion, don't be afraid to do a little product experimenting. Sure, household items can be used as intended, but they can also serve an entirely new purpose as well.

For instance:

- Conditioner is a great alternative to shaving cream

- Shea butter is a wonderful natural moisturizer
- Baking soda works well in lieu of regular tooth-paste

A quick search on Pinterest will give you hundreds of DIY options and homemade mixes to try. I've even seen recipes for homemade deodorant, although to be honest, that one scares me a little bit! You'll tell me if I smell, right?

5. MAKE IT LAST LONGER

You'll get many more applications out of your toiletries if you cut off the tops of squeeze bottles or add a little water to your body wash to get that last little bit out. Joseph and I have an ongoing toothpaste war to see how long we can go before throwing the tube away, and sometimes it gets pretty competitive. But then again, it's amazing how many days, sometimes weeks, we're able to go before replacing the nearly empty tube!

In regards to razors, here's how to extend the life of your blades:

- Dry blades thoroughly after using to prevent rust (blot dry with a towel or blow dry)
- After shaving, soak in baby oil or olive oil to keep rust-free
- Store in a cool, dry place to avoid humidity...and rust (which means the shower is probably a bad idea)
- Run them up and down a piece of denim (ten to fifteen times, opposite the direction you would shave—Joseph swears by this!)

Lastly, there is truth in the saying, "A little goes a long way." Don't feel like you need to use a ton of product to get the results you want. A small pump of lotion covers a bigger area than you might think, and a dollop of body wash quickly lathers from just a few bubbles to more than plenty.

If you have sensitive skin, you know many personal care products can create a host of issues. One look at the ingredient list and it's no wonder! Our skin is our biggest organ and everything we put on top of it soaks right in, including toxic chemicals.

But organic products are more expensive and often have a limited shelf life. It's really hard to find coupons on them too, which is why I go through Grove Collaborative to find the best price. Grove Collaborative is an autoship program that will ship toiletries and other household products right to your door.

Go through my referral link below and get $10 just to try it out!

CreativeSavingsBlog.com/GroveCollab

DAY 22 ACTION PLAN:

- Next time you see a great sale, buy two or three of that item instead of just one. Take advantage of the great deal while you can!

- Check Amazon to compare the prices of your favorite toiletry products. If they're competitive or cheaper than the store, add them to your virtual cart the next time you need a replacement.

- Be conscious about how much product you squeeze out of the bottle. Remember, a little goes a long way!

Day 23:
FIND CLOTHES FOR LESS

I'm not a fashionista by any means, but just like my hair, the right clothes can make or break my confidence. I don't know about you, but I feel so much better when I'm wearing a cute outfit that flatters, rather than something that doesn't fit or look right!

While I would love to splurge on a whole new wardrobe, my frugal nature rebels against paying any more than I have to for a new blouse, skinny jeans, or pair of heels. And if I'm being *really* honest, I'd much rather spend my money on books or a couple home improvement projects to make my house look just a little bit nicer. Because...well, those are simply my priorities right now.

But I'm certainly not opposed to adding a few extra pieces to my closet every now and then, especially now that I've learned how to snag quality items without ever paying full price. I've also changed my buying habits to reflect more of my own style and rely on the brands I love and trust. This alone has saved me from many cases of retail regret, which saves me even more time and money in the long run!

Whether you need a couple new items for yourself, your family is growing out of their clothes faster than you can shop, or you just want to treat yourself to a day at the mall without the guilt, here are five practical tips to remember before you buy. It's time to build a wardrobe you love, and finally achieve that look you want for much less!

1. GET CREATIVE WITH WHAT YOU ALREADY HAVE

It always surprises me how creative I can be with pieces I already have hanging in my closet or stuffed in the back of my dresser drawers. It takes just a little effort to put together, but I've found some new favorite outfits just by stepping outside my comfort zone and pairing items I never would have thought to pair before!

If you're a total fashion newbie like me, you'll probably find it helpful to look at Pinterest fashion boards and magazine outfits for inspiration. The key is to focus on classic pieces, without going too trendy. You can play with trends in your accessories, which are more easily switched out anyway.

Another idea is to create your own capsule wardrobe, often called the minimalist wardrobe because of its limitations in clothing items and colors. But don't let that description fool you. The capsule wardrobe has a ton of potential.

And if you *really* want to get creative, repurpose clothing items that don't fit or you don't like anymore by using them in a completely different way. An old t-shirt can be turned into a trendy top, and a frayed or holey pair of jeans can easily become shorts or capris. Think about how you can use the piece in a different way before you throw it in the trash!

2. STICK TO THE SALE AND CLEARANCE RACKS

My mother taught me almost everything I know about managing my money, and from an early age, my sister and I always knew the clearance section was the best place to find new clothes. Even now, if I can't find anything I like on the clearance rack, I immediately move on to the next store. Sometimes it's hard to pass up other pieces I love, but I know I would regret paying full price later!

However, the clearance rack isn't the only place to find hidden gems. Knowing seasonal sales and markdown schedules gives you a better chance of scoring the sweater you love at a much lower price. Stores are constantly turning over inventory, but right after Christmas and into the New Year, and then again at the end of June are the best times to snag a steal. That's when the big spring and fall collections come out, and you can get huge discounts on anything summer and winter themed.

But let's say there's a clothing item you *really* want. It might be gone by the time the next inventory shipment comes in, and if you truly love it, you can still get the best price simply by understanding the store's retail cycle.

J from JsEverydayFashion.com explains a timeline:[11]

Clothes go on the floor at full retail price. Old stuff is reduced. A few weeks later, new clothes are given a small discount. A few more weeks later, stores get ready for the next shipment and most of the store goes on sale.

It might be a good idea to use a coupon and snag that clothing item you want during its first round of discounts—that is, if there aren't too many left on the rack. Otherwise, you can play it safe and wait a few more weeks for the better deal.

READER TIP:

I have bought NEW clothes multiple times at our local Salvation Army and my mother-in-law and father-in-law always find the cutest new clothes at their thrift stores for all my kids. When I pulled out our winter clothes, I was amazed at how much we had simply from older kids giving us new clothes that didn't fit, birthday clothes that were too big...etc.

—*Christina, CA*

3. DON'T BE AFRAID TO TRY USED

It's easy to be turned off by something that is old, used, and unwanted by someone else. But just because you've had a bad experience at one yard sale, thrift store, or consignment shop, doesn't mean they're all bad. And that's from someone who doesn't particularly enjoy shopping at these places herself!

Here are the things to keep in mind at each venue:

- **Yard Sales** – These are great places to find gently and barely worn kids' clothes. Check Craigslist on Thursday to see where all the sales will be on Friday and throughout the weekend, then head out early for the best picks. Have a piece of paper with you that lists everyone's sizes and measurements so you don't have to remember as you browse.

- **Thrift Stores** – This is another great place to find kids' clothes, and I would also add jeans, dress pants, skirts, and dresses for adults to the mix as well. I usually avoid the shirt section because the quality is not always the best if it's been worn before. The wear and tear of a top that's been stained or stretched doesn't make me feel cute—I don't care how cheap it is. I also don't do used shoes, but that's because it makes me pretty squeamish to think of wearing an item previously on someone else's feet!

It's easy to get overwhelmed at the thrift store, so I recommend sticking to the color palette you know looks good on you and only shopping those sections of the store. Most thrift stores I've been to organize their racks that way anyway. I would also make sure you have enough time and patience to browse. You're more likely to find that gem you've been searching for if you're patient enough to really dig.

• **Consignment Shops** – Consignment shops are a bit different from thrift stores in that they usually sell high quality items that are *slightly* used, and focus on quality brands in a big way. You can also donate your own clothing items and get credit towards another purchase you make in-store.

If at first you don't succeed with used clothing stores, don't give up right away! It all depends on the type of shop and where it's located. Don't be afraid to experiment in another neighborhood or even a nearby city to see if you find better items at even better prices. You never know which wealthy family will donate a few gems from their expensive closet!

READER TIP:

I recently ordered from ThredUp and Schoola and LOVED them! I lucked out and found 50% off codes on both of their Facebook pages, so that really made my money go a long way.

—Kristen, JoyfullyThriving.com

4. BUY ONLINE

In just the past few years, buying clothes online (even used ones!) has become really popular and changed the face of online shopping. ThredUp.com and Schoola.com offer services where you can buy and sell your clothes straight from their website, and they always have huge discounts up to 90% off. I have shopped at ThredUp multiple times, and have always been pleased with the prices and quality. If you'd like to try ThredUp for yourself, you can get $10 to spend by using my referral link:

CreativeSavingsBlog.com/ThredUp

Outside of used clothing, you can also buy brand new items for just as great a deal, if not better, simply by shopping online. While regular sales from the retailer are awesome in themselves, you should also check RetailMeNot.com for coupon codes before submitting the virtual checkout button. Combine the coupon with Ebates.com, and you'll also get cash back!

Don't forget to sign up for your favorite retail store email lists to receive discount codes every month (and around your birthday). Even better, if you leave your online shopping cart full for a few days, the retailer will most likely email you a coupon as an incentive to come back and check out.

5. HOST A CLOTHING SWAP

I have to admit that I've never done a clothing swap before, but this is something I would love to do with my friends in the very near future! There are so many times I feel plain icky or "blah" about my own clothes, even though they would look perfectly acceptable on someone else.

Hosting a party with your friends is the perfect excuse for everyone to declutter their closets and bring clothes they aren't thrilled about wearing anymore, and lets them select a few new pieces without buying new at the store. Make sure you invite women of all shapes and sizes and have everyone drop off their clothes at least a week before the swap so you can get set up and organize clothing by size and category.

You also might want create a few rules, like, "Everyone is allowed to take home as many items as they bring," so everyone gets an equal chance to shop. Don't forget to provide a few snacks too!

Casually shopping for clothes is fun, but I prefer to shop with a plan to make the most of my time and money. One of the things I do to stay on track in the store and online is to have a printable Clothing Inventory and Shopping List with me at all times.

This can be something as simple as a scrap piece of paper or digital note on your smartphone, or you can download the sheet I use at CreativeSavingsBlog.com/ExpenseResources to stay organized as you build a wardrobe you love.

DAY 23 ACTION PLAN:

- Pare down your wardrobe to focus on a specific color palette that will easily mix and match. This makes getting ready for the day and knowing what clothes to buy so much easier!

- Explore different thrift stores and consignment shops in the area to find a favorite. Remember to check stores outside your area too.

- Sign up for your favorite retailers' email lists and start tracking sales cycles so you know exactly when to buy.

Part 7:
Reduce Gifting
Expenses

Day 24:
CELEBRATE BIRTHDAYS ON A BUDGET

Although I'm not a huge fan of getting older (okay, I have a *major* phobia when it comes to aging!), I love everything about birthdays. I look forward to eating my favorite ice cream cake, unwrapping thoughtful gifts, and trying to guess what special activities Joseph has planned for me this year. He definitely spoils me!

But as much fun as birthdays are to have yourself, they are tons of fun to plan for others too. I could spend hours browsing Pinterest and creating themed birthday boards for just about any party. Don't even get me started on all the DIY projects that take your bash to the next level. Put me in charge and you can guarantee I'll go a teensy bit overboard.

As with any celebration, though, there's food to buy, favors to purchase, decorations to coordinate, and activities to plan. If money's no object, sure, it's much easier to just go to the store and buy everything you need without worrying about the cost. But for a frugal girl like me, it's hard to justify spending so much on a one-day event when I have many other goals in mind for my money.

But what if you could have both? You know, host a beautiful birthday party without spending much at all?

These five budget-friendly ideas are proof you can make that happen. Plus, you'll find that the smaller your budget, the more creative you can be. Your next bash may be the best one you've thrown yet!

1. DITCH THE YEARLY PARTY

As much fun as it is to have a party every year, it's not a necessity. My parents were very intentional about our birthday parties, and we were allowed to have two major ones growing up (when we turned six, and then again when we turned thirteen.

While I might have been a little disappointed that my whole class couldn't go bowling or play mini-golf every year, it saved my family a lot of money in the long run and made the birthday parties that we *did* have extra special!

Besides, on the "off" years, you can still make the birthday special by doing an activity that would be too stressful to do with a large group. Or, you can have a special evening out at a favorite restaurant, then come back for cake and ice cream with immediate family.

2. MAKE YOUR OWN CAKE

One of the craziest things I ever did straight out of college was own my own cake business for a couple of years. It was fun while it lasted, but I quickly found out that cake decorating just wasn't my life's passion. The stress of getting brides their cake in one piece, and spending hours with a piping bag in my hand took their toll, and I decided I wasn't cut out for that line of work. Still, I am very thankful I have the skills to create bakery-inspired cakes at home, and guess what? You can do it too!

Not every baked good needs to be *Cake Boss* worthy, but a few basic skills will help you go far. Pretty soon you'll be able to create a simple, but pretty party cake with ease. My favorite way to learn cake decorating techniques is to sign up for a course at A.C. Moore or Michaels, but if you'd rather practice in the comfort of your own home, I recommend a Craftsy.com class.

Even a few dozen cupcakes can look professionally decorated without a lot of effort. My favorite decorating tip to use is 1M from the Wilton collection, and it creates a very pretty swirl on top of each cupcake. Sprinkle with a dusting of colored sugar, and everyone will think you had the local bakery cater your event.

3. PLAN AN INEXPENSIVE MENU

Whether you're planning a meal for a large party or a smaller, more intimate one, don't feel like you have to provide a gourmet dinner for every birthday. A simple soup buffet in the winter or hot dogs and hamburgers in the summer are perfect alternatives to an expensive meal. Shop at discounted grocery stores for the best prices, and go generic when you can. Simple sides, such as seasonal fruit or potato chips are great to have on hand too.

You can also eliminate lunch or supper altogether, and instead provide a table full of inexpensive finger foods topped off with cake and ice cream for dessert. Plan for an after lunch party and wrap up before supper so guests don't expect to be fed a three-course meal. And by all means, let them offer to bring something!

READER TIP:

I use Pinterest to find a lot of DIY ideas and do most of my own invitations and cards.

—Tina, SC

For plates, cups, and utensils, save yourself the hassle and go plastic. The dollar store is the best place to stock up on party supplies, and solid colors are the easiest to use for another potluck or picnic lunch later in the year.

4. DIY YOUR DECORATIONS

There is DIY inspiration everywhere—Pinterest, magazines, blogs—and you don't have to be an expert crafter to try your hand at a few tutorials. All it takes is following simple instructions, and a few dollars in supplies!

For instance, you can:

- Make your own photo props by cutting out printable shapes and attaching them to a straw or popsicle stick. Add a photo backdrop with streamers and fabric.

- Make a paper garland out of scrapbook paper and twine.

- Dip the bottoms of plastic utensils in glue and glitter, then arrange in a mason jar on the food table.

- Cut out a cardboard shape that represents the age the birthday boy or girl is turning, and cover with scrunched tissue paper.

- Attach star-shaped (or any other theme) stickers to the tops of lollipop sticks, and use them in place of an expensive cake topper.

The possibilities are endless when you stop and think about it. But if you don't have time to make your own decorations, a quick trip to the dollar store for party streamers and balloons will turn any space into a party setting for cheap.

5. SIGN UP FOR FREEBIES

Birthdays don't always have to be celebrated at home. In fact, sometimes it's cheaper to go out, thanks to a variety of retail and restaurant birthday freebies! You'll want to sign up for them at least thirty days before your birthday to be eligible, then print and keep on hand to enjoy free stuff throughout your birthday month.

READER TIP:

Firehouse Subs gives you a free sub on your birthday—you don't have to have a coupon or be on their email club—all you need is your ID!

—Eileen, FL

Here are a few of my favorite examples:

- **Auntie Anne's** – FREE pretzel on your birthday. I think the Cinnamon Sugar ones are the best!

- **CVS** – $3 Extra Bucks if you belong to the Beauty Club.

- **Panera Bread** – A surprise on the MyPanera Rewards Card, usually a FREE bakery item or drink.

- **Ulta** – FREE mascara if you're signed up for ULTAmate Rewards.

- **Starbucks** – My Starbucks Rewards gives you a FREE drink or treat. I just love the Double Chocolate Chip Frappuccino!

This is just a sampling of the hundreds of freebies available. You can find an extensive and always up to date list at

CreativeSavingsBlog.com/Birthday

When all's said and done, it's not about how much you spend throwing the best birthday bash you can imagine, it's the memories you make that day that truly count. As long as your birthday prince or princess (or hubby!) feels incredibly special that day, you can stop stressing about the things that didn't go as perfectly as you had imagined. Besides, it'll make for laughable moments later on!

DAY 24 ACTION PLAN:

- Start planning for the next birthday celebration you have by creating a birthday inspiration board on Pinterest. Pin a good assortment of DIY and frugal decorating ideas!

- Learn how to decorate a simple birthday cake by taking a class or watching a few YouTube tutorials.

- Sign up for at least five of your favorite retailers' email lists so you are eligible for FREE stuff during your birthday month.

Day 25:
CUT HOLIDAY SPENDING

The holidays happen at the same time every year, yet we are still caught off guard when we realize Christmas is a little less than a week away. What is supposed to be the most joyous and peaceful season of the year quickly turns into one of stress as we realize all the cookies we need to bake, decorations to put up, gifts to buy (and wrap!), and how much money we have to spend along the way.

Although Joseph and I budget for these types of things, we don't always stay under it. We too get swept up in the advertisements, magazine-worthy gift guides, and enticingly low prices of gifts that weren't in our price range to begin with. The hustle and bustle of the crowds, stores, and ticking time clock don't help that much either.

Before we know it, we're rushing around buying everything we "need," so we can make this Christmas the one to remember. Meanwhile, we stop paying attention to how much it costs, because we just want to get it done as quickly as possible. But those receipts add up, my friend!

If this sounds all too familiar, then it's time to stop shopping without a plan and prep your finances so they don't take such a hit during the holiday season—because they don't have to. You can be smart with where and how much you spend, and still have a gorgeous celebration with money left over. Yep, it's true!

Here are six creative ways to cut costs, *and* create a stress-free holiday:

1. START SAVING NOW

Like I mentioned before, Christmas should not come as a surprise to anyone. It's the same day, in December, every year, and we have 364 days to prep for it—so let's use that time wisely!

I set money aside starting in January—a little from each paycheck—so by the time Christmas rolls around, I know exactly how much money I have to spend on gifts. Then I determine a budget for each person using my Christmas Gift Budget Worksheet, which helps me stay on track throughout the season. You can download a copy at

CreativeSavingsBlog.com/ExpenseResources

READER TIP:

I shop year-round for Christmas gifts—starting for the next year almost as soon as this Christmas is over. That way, I can take my time and find great deals on gifts that I know my family will love.

—Kristen, JoyfullyThriving.com

This strategy is similar to the 52-Week Savings Plan that you may have seen floating around the web or on Pinterest, but instead of the gradual savings increase throughout the year, my method focuses on a fixed amount from January to December. It's much more practical, and creates the savings habit that a gradual increase cannot. Plus, you can customize it to the exact amount you want to save by the end of the year!

Here's an example of how much you could save if you set aside the following amounts every week starting in January:

$10/week = $470 by December

$20/week = $940 by December

$30/week = $1,410 by December

Each of these savings plans is available as a downloadable worksheet at CreativeSavingsBlog.com/ExpenseResources. You'll also find a completely custom plan if you'd like to save a different amount from the ones mentioned above.

2. GET CREATIVE WITH GIFTS

One quote from *The Grinch* has stuck with me as I think about consumerism and Christmas:

> *"Maybe Christmas," he thought, "doesn't come from a store. Maybe Christmas ... perhaps ... means a little bit more."*
> —Dr. Suess[12]

While the Grinch isn't only referring to gifts in his surprisingly profound thoughts, it reminds me that the best gifts are not ones that have to come from a retail shelf in a big box store. They can be creative and come from the heart too. Gourmet goodies, DIY hand scrubs, and other handmade items often hold the most meaning, and they can be pretty thrifty too!

The key to DIY gifts, though, is to start early. Every year I say I'm going to make my gifts for everyone, and then at the last minute I have to rush around trying to gather up ten different gift cards because I simply didn't make time. Start a Pinterest board if you haven't already for DIY gift ideas, then schedule some time each month to work on them.

I also don't think you should be expected to buy, or make, a gift for everyone. Each Christmas, it seems like my own gift list gets larger, but there has to be a stopping point somewhere. Besides, Christmas isn't about gifting, so keep the tradition as something special among immediate family members, and do a Secret Santa exchange with everyone else. This will keep the gifting cost down, and will be less stressful for everyone involved.

3. STOCK UP ON BAKING SUPPLIES

Every year starting in November, grocery stores discount almost all of their baking supplies—that means deeply discounted and stock up prices for us! One week it's flour, the next it's chocolate chips and cake mixes. Each week, take advantage of the sales and store extra ingredients wherever you have room.

Baking supplies usually last a long time, and since most of us use them all year 'round, it makes sense to grab enough to last until Easter. That's usually when the next round of baking supplies goes on sale.

You should also get a head start on holiday baking. Cookies, pies, and all sorts of sweet treats almost always freeze well, and you won't have to spend every waking moment in the kitchen preparing food for your special guests. Plus, if you start early enough, you have the luxury of making goodies as their ingredients go on sale, instead of waiting until the last minute and buying everything at full price.

4. BE SMART ABOUT DECOR

You don't have to spend money on cheaply made decor items that fall apart after the first year you use them. Not when there are so many cute and gorgeous decorating projects on Pinterest anyway! You don't have to be particularly crafty to do them either. Just follow a few simple instructions and have a glue gun close by.

Here are some quick ideas for decor that makes a big impact on your home, not your wallet:

- Print out a cute printable and buy a cheap frame from the dollar or craft store.

- Use fabric scraps on a Styrofoam cone shape to create a pretty Christmas tree.

- Spray paint pinecones and create your own holiday mantle display with lights and a mini village made out of scrapbook paper covered cardboard.

- Put your own touch on a homemade wreath. Buy a few sprigs of greenery, holly berries, and add a festive bow.

You can also scout out deep Christmas discounts for store-bought items if you prefer. Michaels and Hobby Lobby usually have the best sales, and mark down their decor pieces, artificial trees, and other glittering baubles at 50% off during December. After Christmas it goes down to 70%, but the earlier you can go, the better. Last year, Michaels was only down to a few shelves of Christmas supplies *two* days after the holiday!

5. GRAB GIFT-GIVING SUPPLIES FOR LESS

Those sales I mentioned above are not just for decor items; they're for gift-giving too. Stock back up on bows, wrapping paper, and Christmas cards for just pennies, and you'll always replenish your stash by spending hardly a thing. But if you wait too long and miss out on the deep discounts, dollar stores are the best place for tissue paper and bags.

When it comes to gifting presents, it's good to keep various sizes of cardboard and packaging boxes on hand whenever you can find them. Gift bags are fine for big and bulky items, but I always prefer wrapping in a box when I can. I actually have a box of boxes in my closet specifically for this purpose!

Also, if I'm not able to stock up on cards and gift tags after the holidays, I'll comb through my craft supplies to make my own. Simple cardstock, stickers, and creative punches are all you need to create a gorgeous handmade card in minutes.

6. CELEBRATE ON A DIFFERENT DAY (OR WEEK)

Christmas Day is special, not because of the day we celebrate it on, but because of who we celebrate it with. If you live out of town, consider having Christmas as an immediate family, but celebrate it on a different day with extended loved ones. It's less stressful, not to mention much cheaper!

For instance, the year we moved to Florida, we also had a wedding to attend back in NY. That meant we were running low on funds for Christmas plane tickets. Which if you're not used to traveling around the holidays, airplane tickets and fees that time of year can cost a pretty penny.

We decided it would be better, and cheaper, to fly up in early January and celebrate Christmas with my family a week later. No, it wasn't exactly on Christmas Day, but we still had a great time, and saved about $200 *a ticket* on airfare. There's no harm in pushing pack your celebrations for a few days or even weeks. I say you can have Christmas whenever you want to have Christmas!

When you really stop and think about it, the holidays are for remembering the true reason for each and every celebration, and enjoying the limited time you have with family and friends. It's a time to step back and reflect on the past year full of blessings, and look towards new ones with anticipation and excitement.

That means it's more crucial than ever to spend smart during the busy holiday season so you can spend less time thinking about how much money you spent, and more time with the ones you love. You'll have money left over in the New Year too!

DAY 25 ACTION PLAN:

- Print out and plan your Christmas budget with the Christmas Gift Budget Worksheet.

- Keep an eye out for thrifty and creative gift ideas, and tuck them away to give later in the year.

- Go through your gift wrapping supplies and write down what you need to buy for next year. Then keep your eye out for those deep discounts after the holidays are over!

Day 26:
SAVE ON SPECIAL EVENTS

Birthdays and Christmas happen on the same day every year. And since we know they're coming at least 364 days in advance, we're able to plan for them accordingly. But what about the bridal showers, baby showers, weddings, and graduations that pop up in between? Now that's an entirely different story.

Depending on how many you have to attend *and* give a gift for, I know firsthand how incredibly easy it is to blow through all the money you previously set aside for the next birthday and upcoming Christmas holiday. Sometimes it feels just as expensive to be a guest at these events as it is to put them on!

I distinctly remember the year almost everyone we knew was either getting married or having their first baby. Of course we wanted to be there to congratulate and celebrate with them, but by the third or fourth wedding, we were running low on funds. Not just for gifts, but also for all the bridesmaid gowns and tuxedo rentals too.

It made both of us take a step back, talk through, and consider how we would approach these kinds of events in the future. We didn't want to be stingy, and loved showing our support, but was there a way to do both for less?

You bet! These six tips keep your wallet intact *and* help you weather every wedding, shower, and graduation season with class. In fact, you might even find that these kinds of gifts are the most creative and fun to give of all.

1. SET A BUDGET

Any time I feel like my money is spiraling out of control, I know it's time to create a budget for that specific category. So in addition to our budgets for car insurance, groceries, utilities, etc., we now have a category for gifts too. This has saved us from "stealing" from other categories just to cover an upcoming wedding or shower gift!

To figure out how much we'll need to set aside, we estimate how many events we think we might go to in a year. I take the amount we would normally spend for such an event (multiplied by how many events I assume we'll be going to), and add that to my final birthday and Christmas spending totals. Then I take that yearly amount, and divide it according to our bi-weekly paycheck schedule.

Here's an example:

- 2 Weddings ($25 gift each) = $50
- 3 Showers ($20 gift each) = $60
- 2 Grad Parties ($15 gift each) = $30
- Birthdays = $200
- Christmas = $400

TOTAL SPENDING = $740/Year

$740/26 (Bi-Weekly Paychecks) = $28.46

So, I need to set aside approximately **$29** every paycheck to adequately cover all gift-related spending for the year.

Your estimates will probably be completely different from mine, and you may have to adjust it every year, but at least you will have a little extra money set aside so you're not caught completely off guard!

2. BE REGISTRY SAVVY

Gift registries can be such a lifesaver when shopping for the soon-to-be mom or bride. Instead of wondering what they want or need, you know exactly what's on their wish list. But sometimes, this wish list is filled with items well above your budget.

While it's perfectly okay to buy a couple dish towels and kitchen utensils, here are some registry tricks to help you save on some of the bigger items too:

- **Shop the registry elsewhere** – Look at the registry items, but don't feel obligated to buy from that specific store. If they're registered at a place like Bed Bath & Beyond, Macy's, or Target, you can often find the same item for less on Amazon.

  For instance, a Keurig K10 Mini Plus Brewing System costs $79.99 at the big box store, but the same exact model on Amazon rings in at $65.98. That's a $14.01 difference! Just make sure to call the store and have them remove the item from the registry if you do this.

- **Take advantage of a sale** – When you know what stores are on a specific registry, immediately sign up for the store's mailing list and check often to see what sales and coupons they're offering. Sometimes you'll get lucky and be able to snag the winning item for a lot less.

- **Combine forces with friends or family members** – It's always nice to get some of the bigger items like a KitchenAid mixer for the bride, or a car seat for the expecting mama, but if it's not in your budget, grab a few friends or family members and combine your buying power. The benefits are two-fold: the recipient crosses some major items off her wish list, and you have less to think about when shopping for them.

3. MAKE THOUGHTFUL DIY GIFTS

One look through Pinterest, and you'll find hundreds, if not thousands, of gifts you can make for the new mom, bride, or graduate. The possibilities are as limitless as your creativity!

Here are some ideas to get your creative juices flowing.

For Baby:
- Flannel Baby Blankets
- Burp Cloths
- Baby Bibs
- Knitted or Crocheted Baby Booties and Hats

For the Bride:
- Handmade Thank You Notes
- Printable Art with a Favorite Verse or Romantic Quote
- Favorite Recipe Binder
- Etched Casserole Dishes

For the Grad:
- Memory Book

- Coupons Redeemable for Homemade Cookies

- Special Quilt

- Printable Art with a Favorite Verse or Inspiring Quote

I find that handmade gifts are both fun to make and to receive. Just be sure to set aside time to make that item so you don't end up pulling an all-nighter before the big day. Working on your idea soon after you find out about an upcoming wedding or baby shower is best.

READER TIP:

I like to make handmade cards...you never know down the road when a verse you shared or a thought you cared to write down might be just what that person needs even five to ten years from now! I love scenic photography and have taken my own pictures and put verses on them and have them in 5x7 cards that you can frame and hang. I also have asked the graduate for their favorite verses and then incorporate that into the picture.

—Judy, ND

4. GET CREATIVE WITH STORE-BOUGHT GIFTS

If you don't consider yourself to be too handy with the glue gun, buy a few store-bought items, but instead of giving them as they are, try to display them in a creative way. Pinterest is another great place to find ideas, but here are a few quick examples:

For Baby:
- Diaper Cake
- Pamper Basket for Mom
- Onesies with Flair (Embroidery, Iron-on, etc.)

For the Bride:
- Laundry Basket filled with Supplies
- Monogrammed Towels
- Honeymoon Basket

For the Grad:
- Shower Caddy with Personal Care Supplies
- Study Snacks arranged as an "Emergency Kit"
- Tote Bag filled with Office Supplies

Baskets are one of the easiest ways to arrange and personalize a gift. Just think of a theme that would apply to the event you're attending, set a budget, and head to the store for a fun little shopping spree. Best of all, baskets fit every budget. You determine how big or small of a container you want to fill!

5. BUY DISCOUNTED GIFT CARDS

A lot of people think gift cards are too impersonal, but I love receiving and giving them. Besides, new moms and brides-to-be always have items left over on their registry to buy, and graduates love to pick out their own dorm room supplies. A gift card is the perfect solution!

But if you think gift cards always have to be bought at full price, think again. There are plenty of ways to snag a deal and pay less than the gift card is actually worth:

- GiftsCards.com is one of my favorite ways to buy and sell gift cards. There are hundreds of stores listed for varying amounts. When I last looked, a $25 Babies R' Us gift card was going for $22.73. I know a 9% discount doesn't sound like all that much, but when there's no processing fees, and FREE shipping, why wouldn't you save the time and money?

- Another way to buy gift cards is to use your credit card rewards to purchase them. Most credit card companies have a "store" where they offer gift cards in exchange for points. Each month or so, they'll also list a few gift cards on sale, which means you can purchase the card for less than the actual amount.

- Warehouse stores, like Sam's Club, often have a gift card section where you can buy a variety of gift cards lower than their marked value. Sometimes it's just a couple dollars off, but other times they can be quite significant!

- Lastly, buying gift cards around the holidays will give you plenty of bonus gift cards and cash to use later in the year. Most restaurants offer a $25 gift card with a $5 bonus on top of it, and new moms always appreciate not having to think about meals.

6. PURCHASE GIFTS THROUGHOUT THE YEAR

One of the best ways to save on gifts is to purchase them on sale throughout the year. Kitchen outlet stores and Black Friday sales always have appliances and kitchen gadgets for a lot less, and I don't know a bride who can't use another dish towel or spatula.

Clear out a space in your closet dedicated to these kinds of items, and then when you find a sale, pick one up and stash it away. Even simple things like candles and throws are generic and can always be used. The best part is, you'll never be caught off guard by another event again, and everything you purchase will be because you found it on a deeply discounted sale or clearance rack.

Another bonus is the next time someone buys you a Christmas gift and you weren't planning on giving them one, you can go to this closet and pick out something to save face!

The next time you receive an invitation to a baby shower, bridal shower, graduation, or wedding, remember...the most expensive gift does not always equal the most meaningful one. If you play a big part, such as hosting a shower, making the cake, or traveling to a wedding that results in extra hotel and airline fees, it's okay to scale back and not spend as much. Your presence is a gift in itself.

DAY 26 ACTION PLAN

- Start a gifting budget if you haven't already, and estimate how many events you expect per year, as well as how much you intend to spend.

- Clear out a spot in your closet specifically for these kinds of gifts, and keep an eye out during the year for generic items that are the perfect fit.

- Create a Pinterest board specifically for DIY gifts, and pin your favorites to reference later.

Part 8:
Reduce Miscellaneous Expenses

Day 27:

LOWER THE COST OF PET CARE

In a completely different reality, Joseph and I would be living on our own homestead with a few chickens, goats, mini cows, ducks, and at least a couple of rabbits. Obviously, this has yet to happen, because one, the cost, and two, a husband who thinks he will be stuck doing most of the cleanup. And I hate to admit it, but he's probably right!

I guess I'm just as big of an animal lover as the next person—okay, probably a *lot* more—but I do have to say that pets can get pretty expensive. Between food and vet bills, grooming and pet sitting costs, our furry friends deserve their own part of the budget, that's for sure.

Joseph and I have considered adding another rescue bunny to the family, but we know the cost of supplies and possible medical bills will double, and we're not sure we're ready to handle that just yet. We actually fostered an extra rabbit alongside our own for a couple of months when we were first married, and we were shocked at how much more we had to pay for extra supplies!

Plus, in addition to the yearly shots and checkups, as pets get older, they have a higher chance of a medical emergency. We've personally had to make the tough call between an expensive procedure that may or may not work, and giving relief in a different, more humane way.

But a life void of pets is certainly not one I desire to experience, which means the alternative is to cut costs as much as possible. Here are six easy ways to save money on pets, so you can enjoy your playmates and stop worrying about how much you're paying to take care of them:

1. BE PREPARED FOR THE COSTS

With any pet, there are initial costs and maintenance costs, so prepare your budget for both before you go shopping for that little bundle of fur. Grooming, food, and regular checkups are the most important expenses to consider, but don't forget to factor in pet sitting services for when you're away too.

Estimate the monthly cost as best you can, then set aside that amount in preparation for all pet-related expenses. An average starting point is usually between $500-$700 per year for either a dog or cat, but remember, you will have a lot of one-time fees as well. A crate, initial checkup, spaying/neutering fee, litter boxes, and toys will add to that first-time yearly cost.

You'll want to consider having a pet Emergency Fund in place for those middle of the night vet visits that seem to happen at least once or twice during the life of your pet. You can always adjust the amount if needed, but the key is to just *start*!

ANNUAL PET EXPENSES:

Food: Dog $120 | Cat $145

Annual Exams: Dog $235 | Cat $130

Litter: *Cat $200*

Toys and Treats: *Dog $55 | Cat $25*

License: *Dog $15*

Pet Insurance: *Dog $225 | Cat $175*

Miscellaneous: *Dog $45 | Cat $30*

*numbers from the ASPCA

2. ADOPT A MIXED BREED

Purebred fans might hate me for this, but I honestly believe mixed breeds are not only healthier in the long run (i.e., not as many vet bills), but they also cost less to buy upfront. Without getting into too much detail, the gene pool of purebreds has broken down so much over the years (because it's so "pure"), that each breed is known for specific health problems. This results in more vet bills and an animal that often has a shorter life span.

One of my favorite ways to support pet adoption is to go to the local humane society and find a fur-baby his or her forever home. Fees hover around the $50 mark depending on size or type of animal, and many shelters will start you off with supplies and a bag of food. It's much harder to know the past history or heritage of an adopted pet, especially if they are over a year old, but saving a pet from homelessness gives you that warm, fuzzy feeling you can't get anywhere else!

You can also check Craigslist for pets in need of a loving home. Many owners find that they can't care for their pet anymore, and are willing to give or charge a small fee to re-home them. Most come with their own supplies, so it's an inexpensive way to adopt a pet and find out a little bit more about their past history.

3. KEEP THEM HEALTHY

A healthy pet is less prone to emergency vet visits (and therefore, bills), so do what you can to make sure your pet stays in stellar shape. Get the proper amount of exercise for the size and age of your dog, and be careful about slipping Fido scraps from the dinner table. Grooming regularly, trimming nails, and keeping teeth clean all add up and make a difference too.

You'll also want to stay current on all shots and prevention meds. It's much cheaper to pay for these things now, rather than wait until your pet has Lyme Disease, Heartworm, or a much more serious medical problem. If you do have to buy medications every few months, buying online through a site like 1800PetMeds.com can save you loads of cash. Or you can print out the price sheet and see if your vet will match the price. More than likely they will, and you'll avoid extra shipping costs!

Another option to consider is pet insurance. It might seem silly to pay $18-$20 a month on insurance that you may or may not use, but if you're concerned about an expensive vet bill down the road that you might not be able to cover, you'll want to take the precaution now rather than later. From what I've researched, companies like Healthy Paws and Pet Plan have the best reviews.

4. SHOP AROUND FOR FOOD

If you've ever bought pet food at a chain retail pet store, you know the cost is much higher than Walmart or other discount stores. Shop around and compare prices on pet food to see exactly where you should buy. You might be surprised to find some of the cheapest prices are actually online!

We used to buy all our Timothy Hay for our rabbit through Amazon's Subscribe and Save program (before they stopped offering the product, that is), and even though it's just a few cents cheaper than Walmart, it's still super convenient to have pet food shipped straight to our door. You can also look up your preferred brand of pet food online to see if the company offers any coupons. Combine that with a sale and rewards app, and you'll always get your pet's food for cheap.

Another idea is to make store-bought items at home for less. Both dog and cat treat recipes are practically everywhere (hello, Pinterest!), and all you need is a cute cookie cutter. Ingredients are easy to find too. Most involve some combination of peanut butter, banana, yogurt, and flax seed.

5. GROOM THEM YOURSELF

Grooming your pet at home will not only eliminate the tangles and excessive pet hair problems, but it will also save you a lot more money in the long run. Invest in a simple clipper set, watch a few YouTube tutorials, and give it a go.

However, if your pet does not appreciate your taming their mane (and lets you know it!), you might be better off letting a professional handle it next time around. You can still save money at the groomer's by skipping the fancy cut. A "field cut" means they cut the hair the same length over the entire body, saving the groomer time, and you, money.

Trimming nails is another option for you to do at home. For our rabbit, Joseph and I have a system where he holds the squirming bunny, and I quickly go through and clip the nails. We always give a treat afterwards so they don't associate grooming with a completely bad experience. Just be careful about hitting the quick. It's bloody *and* painful!

6. BE SMART WITH SUPPLIES

Like I talked about before, every pet comes with their laundry list of initial (and recurring) supplies. The pet store is probably the most expensive place you can buy them, so check the following places first before you make the final purchase:

- Dollar Stores – Find toys, pet beds, towels, and food bowls for just a dollar.

- Thrift Stores and Yard Sales – Look for crates, cages, scratching posts, collars, leashes, and food bowls.

- Amazon – Since they're the mecca of all online stores, you can find pretty much anything and everything you could ever want or need on Amazon!

Also, don't feel like you have to get everything on the recommended list for your particular pet. With our rabbit, we skipped on the expensive toys and instead, scatter cardboard boxes, toilet paper rolls, and magazines for him to chew on since he seems to like those better anyway. Your pets can "make do" with a lot less than you think they can!

READER TIP:

Check thrift shops and yard sales for dog toys. Kids' stuffed animals without glass, plastic eyes, or other plastic parts are fine to use for dog toys, and the dogs will tear up a thrift shop toy just as fast as a brand new stuffed animal!

—Heather, ME

If you've lived with your pet long enough, you know their habits and routines like the back of your hand. This means you also know when something just isn't right. We have saved hundreds of dollars on vet bills because we were able to research the issue on Google and try a home remedy before the problem became too serious.

But if it truly is a medical emergency, the internet can give you loads of resources so you have some idea of what to expect before you head to the vet's office. At the end of the day, we want to keep our pets as healthy as possible, and that means we need to spend a little money on them when it's truly important. Thankfully, there are lots of ways to do it for less!

DAY 27 ACTION PLAN

- Figure out the monthly cost of maintaining and taking care of your pet, and make sure you have that money set aside to pay for supplies every month.

- Look for an alternative sourcing option for food. Make sure you compare prices at different stores and online.

- Watch a few YouTube tutorials on grooming your particular pet, invest in the right supplies, and try it yourself.

Day 28:
MAKE ENTERTAINMENT AFFORDABLE

Even though I consider myself an extreme homebody (intro-vert, anyone?), I still enjoy the chance to "get away." It's nice to focus on something other than work or the never-ending laundry pile and dishes in the sink. And to be honest, I *need* those little refreshers so I can be productive in all the other areas of my life.

My favorite stress relievers are visits to the beach, long bike rides, a night out at the movies, days spent at county fairs, or strolling along 5th Avenue in downtown Naples. But if it's a night at home, then binge watching Netflix or reading books and magazines from the comfort of my cozy couch top the list, of course!

Lest you think this is ALL our family does, let me assure you that it most definitely is not. But every once in a while, it's nice to spend a Saturday somewhere other than in between mounds of housework.

Thankfully, we've found many activities that end up be-ing low-cost or free, without ever feeling like we're missing out. Our dating years and first few years of marriage were spent living as frugally as possible, and we've since become self-made experts at finding creative ways to entertain our-selves for just pennies. In fact, we *still* do this, because now we have a couple expensive things on our list that we'd like to do someday, and saving in other areas will help make those things happen eventually!

So while a trip to Disney isn't out of the question, there are multiple ways to make your next family activity less expensive. These seven ideas are a great place to start, and will keep your family entertained while you save up for the activities that *do* cost just a little bit more:

1. TAKE ADVANTAGE OF REWARDS PROGRAMS

I'm a huge fan of rewards programs, and love when companies reward us for being loyal to their specific brand. The entertainment industry offers a few programs that are super easy to sign up for, and will reward you in multiple ways.

- **Regal Cinemas Crown Club** – Members of this club earn points towards free admission, snacks, and drinks for every dollar they spend on movie tickets and at the concession counter. We love discovering these little surprises whenever we use our Regal card!

- **AMC Stubs** – This membership does cost $12 a year, but if you go to the movies a lot, it's definitely worth it. Every $100 you spend gives you a $10 reward, and you'll always have free size upgrades on popcorn and soda.

- **Kellogg's Family Rewards** – Submitting receipts for various Kellogg's items you purchase helps rack up points towards gift cards, coupons, and discounts on entertainment. I was able to score a Buy One Get One Free ticket to a nearby zoo, which saved us $20!

- **Hotel Rewards** – Pick one or two hotel chains that you normally stay at when you travel and sign up for their loyalty program if you haven't already. Every night you reserve, you'll earn points that can add up to a free night. Just beware of expiration dates.

If you really want to get serious about earning rewards, you have to get organized. Start a separate notebook or file folder with all the rules for each program you join. I like to print out a rules sheet or FAQ for each program, just so I'm aware of how I earn rewards, when the points expire, and what the program offers in terms of rewards. You can also start a digital file for this in Evernote.

READER TIP:

Recyclebank.com awards points that can be used for local attraction tickets.

—Meredith, DE

2. USE COUPONS AND MEMBER DISCOUNTS

No matter what attraction you'll be visiting, check each business's website or Facebook page for coupons. Joseph and I recently saved $2 on an entrance fee to a local pumpkin festival just by showing a photo of their Facebook promotion on our phones when we arrived.

Groupon and LivingSocial are two other coupon-oriented websites that offer deals on local attractions, sometimes up to 80% off. Bookmark and visit those sites regularly to see what coupons are available. How it works is you buy the pass or service at a discounted rate, then present your Groupon receipt at the ticket counter or gate.

Likewise, if you're a student, teacher, military member, or belong to AAA or AARP, ask if there is a discount off ticket prices or entrance fees for showing your card. It's amazing all the discounts you can get just by being part of an affiliation or specific club.

READER TIP:

I found out last year that outside food is allowed at the Rogers Centre (where our beloved Blue Jays play) so I've been bringing my own snacks. I can't believe how many times I've bought into their $7 popcorn!

—Christine, TheWalletDiet.com

3. BE SMART AT THEME PARKS

If you live close enough to a theme park, zoo, or museum, you might benefit from purchasing an annual pass, especially if you have kids and would like to visit at least twice a year. Last time we were at Busch Gardens, a day pass was $90 a person, and Disney World just increased their rates to $105. Annual passes are much more cost-effective, and become even cheaper the more you visit.

If you're buying a family pass, you'll probably also want to buy one of the park's special cups for discounted refills. These are usually $5-$10 per cup for your very first purchase, but only $1-$2 a refill. This is a great deal since sodas and food in general are so expensive anyway. Just wash the cups at home and bring them with you every time you visit.

Also, taking food into parks can be taboo, but sometimes they let you through with a few snacks anyway. While I think it's okay to splurge on outside meals if you've budgeted for them, we prefer to save by packing our own and avoiding the greasy food that's bound to make us sick on the next roller-coaster!

4. CHECK THE COMMUNITY CALENDAR

One look at your local newspaper or city website, and you'll find tons of free events available in your community. Find the community calendar and put a few activities on your list to do as a family. Many are free, but the ones that do cost money are sometimes only a few dollars apiece.

Examples of community events are:

- Nature Walks
- Movies in the Park
- Local Festivals
- 5K's
- Parades
- Family Fun Nights

If you live in a college town, the benefits are even better. Sometimes you can even get free admission to art museums and college games!

5. USE YOUR LOCAL LIBRARY

Don't forget to visit your local library for even more fun and savings. The library is so much more than just books, and offers quite a few services and activities that are available for free to the public. Joseph and I use our library every week (sometimes multiple times a week!), and are continually amazed by all the events they have running.

Here are nine free things you can often do at your library:

- **Join a Book Club.** If you're not already involved in a book club, there is usually one happening at the library, or you'll find a bulletin board that lists public groups around the area. It might be a chance to read a new book, or discuss an old one.

- **Take Your Kids to Storytime.** Do something different for the morning or afternoon and go to the library for a story. Sometimes they even have famous authors come for a visit!

- **Learn a New Skill.** Local craft groups will often meet once a month at the library and anyone is welcome to join. Learn how to knit, quilt, make jewelry, or weave a basket.

- **Research Your Family's History.** If you grew up around the area, you'll find documents to help trace your ancestry. Plus, there's always fascinating stuff in the archives about your hometown you might not see anywhere else.

- **Check Out a DVD.** Redbox is pretty cheap, but sometimes you can borrow the same film for less. I know our library has an extensive collection of movies—old and new.

- **Check Out an Audiobook.** It's getting harder and harder to find time to sit down and read actual books. Listening to audiobooks in the car or on your phone during a workout is one way to get in more reading time.

- **Book a Meeting Room.** Most larger libraries have one or two meeting rooms available for book clubs, presentations, conferences, and local events. It would be the perfect place to host your next "business meeting" or "mom to mom" get together.

- **Use the Free Wireless.** In this internet age, it almost seems impossible not to be connected. If you need a change of scenery, or want to avoid a home internet bill, use the library!

- **Read Free eBooks.** Browse your library's database of eBooks and check one out right on your computer. All you need to do is download it to one of your devices and enjoy during the loan period.

Not every weekend has to be filled with an expensive outing to the zoo, stadium, or shopping mall when you have a library nearby. It's thrifty, educational, fun, and best of all, FREE.

6. EXPLORE DISCOUNTED WEBSITES

Whether you want to find a new book to read, watch a movie, catch up on a TV series, or listen to the latest tunes, there are websites where you can do it for much less. And yes, they are all completely legal!

- **For Books** – Sign up for alerts from sites like BookBub.com and BookGorilla.com for epic discounts or even free books. You can also legally download books at Gutenberg.org as a result of expired copyrights. And of course, check the free section of Amazon.com for the latest titles.

- **For Movies** – Netflix is the cheapest and best subscription service with a wide range of flicks for every taste; you'll just need a streaming device to play it. (See Chapter 13 for details). Amazon Prime is more expensive, but also comes with a lot more perks.

- **For TV Shows** – Netflix and Hulu come in at the top again, although Sling TV is another great alternative for live TV channels that don't require a cable package.

- **For Music** – I'm a pretty big Pandora fan, but you'll want to check out AccuRadio and Spotify too. All are free—you just have to be prepared for a few ads here and there. Amazon Prime will also allow you to download your own music for as long as you are a member.

If you do stumble across a less than stellar site, your #1 priority is to be careful! Many freebie sites have malware embedded in them and inappropriate ads that pop up all over your screen. It's best to leave those alone so you are completely protected.

7. ENTERTAIN YOURSELF AT HOME

The word entertainment does not automatically mean a day or night *out*. We have just as much fun playing a family board game, doing a puzzle together, listening to podcasts, or watching a rented movie with homemade popcorn on the stove.

Take it a step further and host a cookout in your backyard, or a fun picnic on the living room floor. The possibilities are endless if you take the time to be a little creative!

Since we can't always do every activity that comes along (whether it's because of time or budget restraints), the best alternative is to determine what is a priority for your family—movies, travel, theme parks, etc.—then put your Entertainment budget towards those specific activities.

You might not be able to do as many of them, and as often, but when you save up enough to afford a special treat every now and then, I guarantee everyone in the family will appreciate it that much more!

DAY 28 ACTION PLAN

- Sign up for reward programs from your favorite movie theaters, nearby attractions, and hotels.

- Check the community calendar for local events happening in the upcoming months, then add a few of them to your weekly schedule.

- Visit your library and explore the events and activities it has to offer. Consider joining a book club or borrowing a movie the whole family would enjoy.

Day 29:
CUT THE COST OF CLEANING SUPPLIES

Cleaning is not my strong suit. In fact, I've seriously considered hiring a house cleaner to do all the dusting, mopping, and vacuuming for me, but my frugal nature does not even want to consider hiring out something I can, and definitely should be doing myself. (Note: This does not mean I have a problem with others using a cleaning service...at least not as long as you can happily afford one!)

The thing is, I know what the power of a clean home can do. It improves my mood, makes me happier, and I'm much less stressed living in a tidy and well-kept home. The problem is, because I don't particularly enjoy this task (like, *at all*), I always spend way too much on cleaning supplies that promise a clean home without the backbreaking effort.

You know what I'm talking about, right? Shower sprays that promise to wipe away soap scum without scrubbing, or dishwasher packs that leave glasses sparkling and crystal clear. I also get swayed by pretty packaging and all things organic and non-toxic. Who wants to inhale cancer-causing fumes? Not me. So even if my cleaning isn't fun, at least the storage baskets under my sink are filled with extremely organized and gorgeous looking bottles!

But all those products are incredibly expensive to purchase, and hardly necessary. Despite what the labels in the cleaning aisle promote, you don't need separate cleaners for the sink, floors, showers, and counters. Nor do you have to spend hours clipping coupons to score brand-name products for free.

These four tips show you how to save time and money as you vacuum, scrub toilets, mop the floors, and wipe away grime in all crevices and corners of your home. You can spend less and still create the crumb-free, germ-free haven you crave!

1. MAKE YOUR OWN

The biggest way you can save on cleaning supplies is to make your own from scratch using everyday household ingredients. White vinegar, borax, rubbing alcohol, baking soda, dish soap, and water can do wonders when mixed in the appropriate measurements. Plus, you can find all sorts of empty spray bottles in different sizes at the dollar store.

Pinterest is filled with DIY knockoffs for just about every cleaning solution available, but here are a few of my favorite recipes:

Streak-Free Window Cleaner

- 1/3 cup white vinegar
- ¼ cup rubbing alcohol
- 3½ cups water
- 1 clean 32-ounce spray bottle

Multipurpose Cleaner

- 1½ pints water
- 1/3 cup rubbing alcohol

- 1 tsp clear household ammonia
- 1 tsp mild dishwashing liquid
- ½ tsp lemon juice
- 1 clean 32-ounce spray bottle

Upholstery Cleaner

- 6 Tbsp soap flakes
- 2 Tbsp borax
- 2 cups boiling water

*Mix soap flakes and borax together in a bowl, slowly add boiling water and stir until smooth. Let cool, then whip into a foamy consistency. Brush suds onto furniture with a bristle brush and scrub away with rag.

Furniture Polish

- 1 cup olive oil
- 1/3 cup lemon juice
- 1 clean 16-ounce spray bottle

Laundry Detergent

- 3 Tbsp borax
- 3 Tbsp washing soda
- 3 Tbsp Dawn dish soap
- Water
- 1 clean gallon container

*Pour borax, soda, soap, and 4 cups boiling water into container, then stir and let cool. Fill the rest of the container with cold water. Use ½ - 1 cup per load, depending on size.

It will take a little trial and error to see what combinations you like best, and what cleans the best, but the total cost of making your own products is pennies compared to what you buy in the store. It's a lot more eco-friendly too!

2. SHOP ONLINE

One of the things I love about today's day in age is the ability to shop online. It's not just for clothes anymore—cleaning supplies, paper products, and even groceries can now be delivered straight to your home.

I've been a member of the Amazon Subscribe and Save program for a couple of years, and it's one of my favorite ways to save on all the household supplies I need to make my home run as smoothly as possible. Basically, you shop the Subscribe and Save store and add different household items to your account that are then sent to you on a recurring basis at a 5% discount.

Some items (like toilet paper) I have coming every month, and my dishwasher tablets come every three to four. The more subscriptions you add to your account, the more you save across the board. Last I checked, five subscriptions gave you a 15% discount on all items!

For a cheaper source of organic and non-toxic supplies, sign up for Grove Collaborative. This company sends a box of goodies to your door whenever you place an order online, and lets you know when it's time to order a refill. It's super convenient and prices are comparable to the brands you would find at Target.

I have personally fallen in love with their Method Hand Soap (after your first purchase you can buy liquid refills that are much cheaper than buying another bottle), Mrs. Meyer's Cleaning Spray, and Method Laundry Detergent. Use my referral link and get $10 off your first purchase:

CreativeSavingsBlog.com/GroveCollab

3. REPLACE YOUR PAPER PRODUCTS

I'm a huge fan of paper towels, but using them to do ALL your cleaning finishes up a roll incredibly fast, not to mention it fills garbage bags and landfills with unnecessary trash. I use them pretty exclusively when I'm cleaning in and around the toilet, but for other less germy jobs, old rags are the perfect reusable alternative.

My favorite way to make our own rags is to cut up old t-shirts, towels, and blankets, and store them neatly folded on a shelf in my laundry room. I use these for dusting, wiping up spills, and as floor, tub, and sink rags as needed. Then I just throw them in the wash when I'm finished.

For kitchen counters and wiping down table crumbs, I have a few store bought dishcloths, but I also recommend homemade crocheted or knitted cloths as well. At first, I was really afraid to use them (I didn't want to ruin all the hard work put in!), but I actually like the way they clean much better than the store-bought brands. You can find easy dishcloth tutorials online, or buy a book on Amazon and learn how to make your own. I love keeping my hands busy knitting while I'm watching one of my favorite TV shows.

READER TIP:

I used to make my own all-purpose cleaner (countertops, windows, etc.) but now I only use Norwex cloths—these are antibacterial cloths that just use water, and cut down on paper towels as well as chemical cleaning supplies. They are amazing and I was super skeptical about them at first. My mom sent me some to try and now I'm hooked!

—Elizabeth, PA

4. DON'T FALL PREY TO RETAIL MARKETING

One of the things I mentioned at the beginning of this chapter was how easy it is to fall prey to pretty packaging and sleazy marketing. As brands release more and more cleaning products for you to buy, and for very specific tasks, you feel compelled to try them in an effort to see if they would work a lot better than the products you already have. At least that's how I always feel!

But a good cleaner can do wonders for sinks, tubs, toilets, floors, cabinets, and much more. It just might take a little trial and error to find your favorite. Also, don't completely disregard store brands until you've tried them. Many times, they're the same quality ingredients as bigger brands, but packaged in a different, less expensive way.

The last thing is to always measure your cleaning products, or at least not use as much. For example, most makers of laundry detergent count on consumers filling the entire cap with liquid, even though the directions on the back call for much less. This wastes the product, and in turn, encourages you to buy more. I actually kept track of one full container of detergent from beginning to end, using the proper amount, and squeezed out significantly more loads than what was promised on the label!

Just a few product swaps and a focus on minimal waste will go a long way in shrinking the cost of your cleaning supplies. And since you use these products almost every day, being careful about what you buy and how much you spend is crucial to keeping this part of your budget under control.

Thankfully, you can do both without cutting any cleaning power!

DAY 29 ACTION PLAN:

- Look up one or two DIY cleaning recipes on Pinterest (or use one of the recipes I've listed here), and make the switch.

- Search for your favorite brand-name cleaning supplies on Amazon Subscribe and Save and/ or Grove Collaborative and see if they offer a cheaper price.

- Take note of how many paper towels you use in a day, and choose to use a rag instead.

Day 30:
SAVE ON HOME OFFICE SUPPLIES

Some girls go crazy over fashion accessories, feel-good chick flicks, and cuddly baby pudge. But me? I geek out over home office supplies. Joseph knows there's nothing that speaks to my heart like a good set of pens and Post-It notes!

At first, it doesn't seem like office supplies could be too expensive, especially since the majority of them cost under $5 apiece. And really, how often do you have to replace pens and paper pads when you can get those for free at vender and county fairs?

But when you factor in bulk paper reams, printer ink, and dare I say pens that actually write, it's easy to go overboard at your local office supply store, or for me...in two specific aisles at Target. Someone tell me why there are always so many notebooks and sticky pads in the most adorable prints and colors?!

It tempts me to buy *way* more items than I actually need. But I guess that's kind of the point.

Whether you're stocking your own supply cabinet at home, filling your child's backpack for school, or starting a home business that requires more file folders than you ever thought possible, these five tips make sure you repurpose, reuse, and be smart about what you buy:

1. BE STINGY WITH PAPER

Limiting paper use is not just good for your wallet, it's essential for the environment too. Just think about how many pieces of paper you use, print, or handle in a given day. Paper is literally everywhere, including our landfills!

The two biggest culprits are the papers we print, and the papers we write on. For your printer, I strongly encourage you to go paperless and only print what you absolutely need, when you absolutely need it. Trust me, I know this habit is hard to break! But you end up not only wasting more paper, you also create unnecessary paper clutter that is overwhelming to deal with when it's spread all over your desk and stacked in piles on the floor.

Evernote is my lifesaver for housing most everything in a paperless setting. I talk a lot more about Evernote and two resources I recommend reading if you're just getting started at

CreativeSavingsBlog.com/OrganizeMyLife

On the flip side, when you *do* have to print out something and you don't need to reference the information anymore, place the paper in a pile that you deem "scrap printer paper." I use my scrap pile to print coupons, my weekly meal plan, and anything else that doesn't require a professional printing.

For smaller pieces of paper, cut your scrap pile into quarters and keep as a stack on your desk to use whenever you need to write a to-do list or quick note. I also use the top half of cards I receive in the mail. This is one of my favorite ways to repurpose handwritten notes that I don't need to keep. It gives each card a second life, plus I always have a cute image on the back of my notes!

READER TIP:

I just bought an HP printer through Best Buy and they have a new program where you pay $2.99 a month for fifty pages per month (with rollover) and they send you new ink. You can do higher ones too depending on what you print. I figure for $36 a year, that's cheaper than one cartridge.

—Jenna, VT

2. SAVE ON INK

Whether you have an inkjet printer or a laser one, the cartridges inside can cost a pretty penny. For our color laser printer, we pay $60-$80 per cartridge, and when we need four of them, we spend well over $200 in one shopping trip!

A lot of people use recycled ink/toner to cut this cost, and if you had asked me a year ago, I would have recommended it too. But the more I use recycled toner (at least from all the brands I've tried), the more I'm dissatisfied long term with the results.

The products generally start out okay, but then they goop up the inside of my printer or leave colored streaks on all my pages. I've never had this problem whenever I've bought a brand new cartridge, which is why despite the price, I tend to buy exclusively new. However, if a reader-recommended site came across my desk, I would definitely be willing to try again!

Here are my three favorite places to buy new cartridges:

• At Staples, you get up to 5% cash back on every purchase, including ink, as well as $2 for every ink cartridge you recycle. Psst...there's almost always a sale or rebate on printer paper too!

- Through Office Depot, you get 10% cash back on ink purchases, plus points equal to approximately $2 for every ink cartridge you recycle.

- At Amazon.com, cartridges can be up to $10 cheaper, which, depending on price, makes it a better deal than your local office supply store— even with the cash back percentage.

Another way to make the ink you use last a lot longer is to print only what you need, print it in black and white, and print only in draft mode. For a laser printer, this doesn't really matter all that much, but for inkjets, it makes a huge difference when you don't need professional quality!

READER TIP:

We have used SuppliesOutlet.com for a few years now with no problems. They have great prices!

—Kelly, NY

3. GO BACK-TO-SCHOOL SHOPPING

Kids or no kids, the back-to-school shopping season is filled with low-priced office supply opportunities! July through August is the best time to stock up on pens, pencils, highlighters, notebooks, rulers, white out, and everything else you can think of to help you be more productive in the office.

The best way to take advantage of this season is to grab a few circulars, head to your preferred store, and ask if they will match their competitors' sales prices. Most will do this, including Target and Walmart, and you'll avoid running from store to store trying to score the latest deals.

The key is to stock up on everything you need to last you until next year, when you can venture out and stock up again. Office goodies are never as low priced as they are during the back-to-school season, so it pays to head out and see what you can find!

4. RAID THE DOLLAR STORE

Any other time of year, the dollar store is one of the best places to find discount office supplies. My favorites to pick up there are index cards, folders, notebooks, and poster board. It sure beats the $3-$4 options found at Target and Walmart!

The dollar store's quality will be a little hit and miss, but you'll soon figure out which supplies are okay to buy there and which ones you should splurge on a little bit. For instance, I refuse to buy sticky notes outside the Post-It brand, because they either don't stick at all, or rip when I'm trying to use the next available sheet.

For other dollar-specific items, don't forget to check the Michaels and Target dollar sections. They both have some really cute note cards, stickers, and paper pads, and the quality isn't bad at all.

5. USE WHAT YOU HAVE

How many times have you gone out and bought new office supplies because you either couldn't find what you already owned, or it wasn't cute enough? Believe me, I'm totally guilty of this! It's surprising how many pens, pieces of paper, and binder clips we find around our home if we take the time to get organized and really look.

I would encourage you to set aside a few minutes to organize what you have, and I promise you'll see right away how much easier it is to find something when it's labeled properly. You'll avoid going to the store *and* won't waste time searching for a supply you already have at home. It's a win-win!

For those extra supplies you don't need right away, keep them stored in a decorative box in your home office or closet. Whenever you run out of an item, be sure to check that box first, before heading out to replace what you need. This is also where you can store those extra back-to-school supplies you stocked up on during August and September.

Home office supplies generally don't take up a huge portion of the budget, and most of us probably don't even have a separate spending category for them—I just group mine in with a section called "Everything Else." But that also means this expense often floats around in your budget unchecked, which can result in an unexpected spending problem down the road if you're not careful.

However, with simple planning around the right times of year, being smart about repurposing, and then using what you already have, you can cut this expense down to something that's extremely manageable. In fact, you might not even notice that it's there at all!

DAY 30 ACTION PLAN:

• Start a "Scrap Printer Paper" pile and use it every time you need to print something not as important. Better yet, see if you can get away with not printing at all!

• Check Amazon.com for the ink or toner cartridge your printer uses and compare prices at Staples and Office Depot.

• Set aside twenty minutes to round up all the office supplies in your home, and organize them in one place. Invest in a couple small storage boxes, if needed.

Day 31:
WHAT TO DO NOW

Congratulations! You've officially made it to the end of *31 Days*! As you've taken this journey, I hope you've realized just how possible it is to reduce your overall spending. Insurance rates aren't set in stone, utilities fluctuate depending on how much you use them, and it's totally doable to cut your cable bill and never miss one of your favorite shows.

But the savings you've discovered along the way are only the beginning. Now it's time to roll up your sleeves and maintain the progress you've made. To continue mastering your expenses, you need to apply these principles every day, and remember to keep a constant eye on your spending so you don't revert back to old habits.

This means you need to keep this guidebook handy. Store it right beside your financial notebook, on a shelf above your office desk, or front and center on your eReading device. I find mine especially helpful as a reminder whenever I update my finances, or to flip through when an unexpected expense pops up and sends me back to the drawing board.

In fact, you may find it helpful to make this exercise a habit every few months as expenses have an uncanny way of increasing when you least expect it. Schedule a "check-in" on your calendar for 31 days from now so you don't forget. You can choose to go through all 31 days again, or flip through and focus on one target area for a full month. Whatever you do, don't give up when the going gets tough. Remember, you have exactly the right tool at your disposal!

HOW TO USE THOSE EXTRA SAVINGS

Now that your budget is a hundred times healthier (I hope quite literally!), you're in a really exciting place. You have choices, and choices mean lots of possibilities for the future.

In my own life, *31 Days* has given me the ability to buy some of those big-ticket items I've been eyeing for our home, helped me plan a regret-free weekend away during the summer, and inspired me to knock out my mortgage even faster. Think about what you want to do with your extra savings as a result of the effort you've put into this challenge.

If you need a place to start, here's what I suggest:

- **Build an Emergency Fund** (or increase the one you already have). If you don't have an Emergency Fund at all, set a goal of $1,000, and put as much money toward it as you can. If you already have a $1,000 fund set aside, add more cushion to it. A good rule of thumb is three months' worth of expenses so you'll never be caught off guard with a financial hardship.

- **Pay off as much debt as you can.** Now that you aren't paying as much towards living expenses, you have extra money to aggressively tackle any outstanding debt—this means credit cards, school loans, car payments, medical bills...even your mortgage! Get that debt GONE.

- **Save towards something you really want.** I strongly believe in the principle of intentional spending, which means you cut back in key areas to spend more on what really matters. Think about what really matters to you, and write down any financial goals that you want to accomplish in the coming year. Now's your chance to finally make them reality!

I hope *31 Days to Radically Reduce Your Expenses* has helped you take back that financial control I know you have hidden inside of you. Your financial future awaits!

ONLINE RESOURCES

This book includes many printable worksheets and resources to supplement your *31 Days to Radically Reduce Your Expenses* journey. All links and printables mentioned are conveniently listed at the following URL:

CreativeSavingsBlog.com/ExpenseResources

ABOUT THE AUTHOR

Kalyn Brooke is the founder of the popular frugal lifestyle blog, *CreativeSavingsBlog.com*, where she empowers women to make their money work smarter, so they can create the life they really want. She strongly believes in pinching dollars over pennies, buying quality products over cheap substitutions, and living a life rich with purpose and intention....not deprivation.

Kalyn has been featured on *BuzzFeed*, *WINK News*, *Good Housekeeping*, *MoneySavingMom.com*, *Times of the Islands* Magazine, and *LivingWellSpendingLess.com*. Originally from Upstate NY, she now resides in sunny Southwest Florida with her husband Joseph and one terribly spoiled rabbit named Cody.

NOTES

1. "Parkinson's Law" Def. 2. *Merriam-Webster Online.* Merriam Webster, n.d. Web. 08 Mar. 2016.

2. "Additional Payment Calculator." *Mortgage Calculators Plus.* n.d. Web. 08 Mar. 2016. <https://www.mortgagecalculatorsplus.com/calc-additionalpayment.php>.

3. Benton, Michael. "Death of Benjamin Franklin." *Benjamin Franklin Bio.* N.p., 06 Nov. 2013. Web. 10 Mar. 2016. <http://benjaminfranklinbio.com/death-of-benjamin-franklin/156/>.

4. "Gas Mileage Tips." *U.S. Department of Energy.* n.d. Web. 08 Mar. 2016. <http://www.fueleconomy.gov/feg/drive.shtml>.

5. "Showers and Showerheads." *Keystone Energy Efficient Alliance.* n.d. Web. 09 Mar. 2016. <http://www.energywisepa.org/category/fact-sheet-categories/water/showers-and-showerheads>.

6. Layton, Julia. "5 Energy Hungry Appliances." *How Stuff Works.* N.p., 29 June 2009. Web. 9 Mar. 2016. <http://science.howstuffworks.com/environmental/green-tech/sustainable/5-energy-hungry-appliances.htm>.

7. "Cleaning Up a Broken CFL." *EPA.* N.p., 26 Oct. 2015. Web. 09 Mar. 2016. <http://www2.epa.gov/cfl/cleaning-broken-cfl#instructions>.

8. Muccio, Craig. "Do Light Dimmers Really Save Energy?" *FPL Blog.* FPL, 11 June 2012. Web. 09 Mar. 2016. <http://www.fplblog.com/energy-efficiency/do-light-dimmers-really-save-energy/>.

9. Carnette, Jamal. "The Average American Pays This Amount For Cable." *The Motley Fool.* N.p., 01 Feb. 2015. Web. 09 Mar. 2016. <http://www.fool.com/investing/general/2015/02/01/the-average-american-pays-this-amount-for-cable-ho.aspx>.

10. Staff. "Drug Samples Are Becoming a Thing of the Past." *DrugWatch.* N.p., 5 Apr. 2012. Web. 09 Mar. 2016. <http://www.drugwatch.com/2012/04/05/drug-samples-become-a-thing-of-the-past/>.

11. "How to Save Money on Clothes." *J's Everyday Fashion.* N.p., 29 Nov. 2012. Web. 9 Mar. 2016. <http://jseverydayfashion.com/2012/11/how-to-save-money-on-clothes.html>.

12. Dr. Seuss. *How the Grinch Stole Christmas.* New York: Random House, 1985. Print.

51284626R00158

Made in the USA
Lexington, KY
18 April 2016